Contents

Introduction

Do you love movies as much as I do? Well, obviously as you bought this book. I am going to keep this intro short and sweet so you can start binging.

I put the most comprehensive compilation of films that are either the best according to the Academy Awards, other movie lists, and my own personal favorites. There are over 1,300 movies to choose from, so have at it.

I have also included fun facts, goofs, some of my favorite one-liners, some we always misuse when quoting, and little tidbits I have found out through watching.

I was going to put where you could watch all these magnificent masterpieces for free, but then I realized after watching *The Girl with the Dragon Tattoo* on Netflix, that they expire and are constantly switching platforms. So, I just included the various platforms and how much each of them costs. If you can't find a movie on a platform, look on IMDB.com or Google. If you have an Amazon Firestick, search on the home panel. Roku might do that as well, I don't remember.

Most of the old classic movies you can probably find on Turner Classic Movie channel with your cable subscription. There are very few movies that aren't even available to rent on Amazon. Does Netflix still rent DVDs? Maybe they will be in the bargain bin at your local Wal-Mart. Also, a lot of movies before 1960 have weird copyrights so you can find them on YouTube for free.

Side Note: I didn't put documentaries in here as most are political and don't want to upset my fan base of either side of the coin.

The Different Apps

Prime Membership: $119 for the year. If you are a student with a valid email address, you get Prime free for six months! Also, after that it's only $59 a year.

Netflix: Netflix has three plans Basic is $8.99 a month, Standard is $13.99 a month, and Premium is $17.99 a month. It ranges because of how many TVs you want it on.

Hulu: It is $5.99 a month with ads, and $11.99 a month without ads. It also offers deal on Cable.

Tubi: This is a free app you can download on your smart tv. Downside is you do have to sit through commercials.

Paramount+: They offer a 7-day free trial, and then it would be $5.99 with limited commercials, and $9.99 a month commercial free.

HBO Max: This membership includes all the HBO channels plus anything from Warner Brothers new releases. It is $9.99 with ads and $14.99 a month without. They do offer a free trial.

Starz: This membership has a 7-day free trial. It is only $2.99 a month for six months if you have a Prime membership, otherwise it is usually $8.99 a month.

IMDB TV: This is free with ads. It will be right on your Prime account or you can download the app.

AMC+: This membership has a free trial. It is $8.99 a month and includes AMC, IFC Films, Shudder and Sundance Now.

FXNOW: It's free to download, but you will have to sign in through your TV provider. Some content may be able to view without doing that.

Pluto TV: This is a free app you can download from your smart tv, Roku, or Firestick. Downside is you will have to sit through commercials, and for some odd reason this one has A LOT of them.

Showtime: This membership offers a whole month free, then only $4.99 for the next three months, but then goes all the way up to $10.99 a month.

TBS: It's free to download, but you will have to sign in through your TV provider. (This might be included in HBO Max membership as well.)

Epix: There is a free trial for this subscription and then it is $5.99 a month.

Cinemax: This has a free trial and is $9.99 a month. This for some reason is not included in HBO Max…

Broadway Channel: This channel has a free 7-day trial, and then is $8.99 per month after that.

Bravo Now: It's free to download, but you will have to sign in through your TV provider.

Eros Now: This app has a free 14-day trial and then $7.99 a month.

Freeform: It's free to download, but you will have to sign in through your TV provider.

FreeTime: This is on Prime and costs $2.99 per child and $4.99 per month for everyone else. If you aren't in prime it's $6.99 per child and $9.99 per everyone else per month. I would research this one, as I think only one or two movies from the list are on it. I don't know if I would waste your money.

Cohen Media Channel: This has a 7-day free trial, and then $4.99 a month. Again, I didn't see too many movies on the list there, so research before purchasing.

MUBI: This has a 7-day free trial, then $10.99 per month. It looked like it had discounted rates for students.

Brown Sugar: This has a 7-day free trial, and then $3.99 per month after that.

Shout! Factory TV: This is available on Amazon for $2.99 a month. I think there was only one movie on this list that was on there. So, if you really want that one movie, I would just rent it, and save yourself the cancellation headache.

YouTube: Yes, YouTube has a lot of movies uploaded there that are in Public Domain, including our channel "The Ultimate Book Club."

There may be more free movie apps or TV networks with apps that I forgot, shoot them over to me if you have favorite that I missed. Find me on Instagram @yourdatingunexpert. My DMs are open!

Academy Awards

Best Motion Picture

If you are going to be a movie guru, you have to watch the Best Motion Pictures winners of the Academy Awards. Although, I feel the selections have went downhill over the past few years, the beginning of the list is amazing and are instant classics.

In 1927, the Academy of Motion Picture Arts and Sciences (AMPAS) was established by Louis B. Mayer, the founder of the Louis B. Mayer Pictures Corporation, which then would be joined into Metro-Goldwyn-Mayer (MGM). Mayer's purpose in creating the award was to unite the five branches of the film industry, including actors, directors, producers, technicians, and writers. Mayer commented on the creation of the awards "I found that the best way to handle filmmakers was to hang medals all over them... If I got them cups and awards, they'd kill them to produce what I wanted. That's why the Academy Award was created."

Mayer asked Cedric Gibbons, art director of MGM, to design an Academy Award trophy. Nominees were notified through a telegram in February 1928. In August 1928, Mayer contacted the Academy Central Board of Judges to decide winners. However, according to the American director King Vidor, the voting for the Academy Award for Best Picture was in the hands of the AMPAS founders: Mayer, Douglas Fairbanks, Sid Grauman, Mary Pickford, and Joseph Schenck.

The list starts from the most recent all the way down to the first Academy Award winners. I hope you enjoy!

- ☐ **Nomadland (2021):** A woman in her sixties, after losing everything in the Great Recession, embarks on a journey through the American West, living as a van-dwelling modern-day nomad. **Goof:** Swankie says she has the book "Final Exit," by Jack Kevorkian. Although it may have been a deliberate error and could be incorrectly regarded as a goof, the book was written by Derek Humphry. He makes some references to Kevorkian and even has a chapter on him, but Kevorkian did not write or help write the book.

☐ **Parasite (2020):** Greed and class discrimination threaten the newly formed symbiotic relationship between the wealthy Park family and the destitute Kim clan. **Goof:** Those who find it unbelievable that homeowners wouldn't notice an entire family living in their basement, will be even less likely to believe that they also wouldn't notice an entire couch missing from their living room. But that's exactly what happens in Bong Joon Ho's "Parasite." Mid-movie, one of the two couches the Parks have disappears and never reappears, and no one seems to think twice about it.

☐ **Green Book (2019):** A working-class Italian-American bouncer becomes the driver of an African-American classical pianist on a tour of venues through the 1960s American South. **Fun Fact:** The real Tony Lip is best known for playing Carmine Lupertazzi on *The Sopranos* (1999) and has had roles in several Martin Scorsese movies.

☐ **The Shape of Water (2018):** At a top-secret research facility in the 1960s, a lonely janitor forms a unique relationship with an amphibious creature that is being held in captivity. **Fun Fact:** Guillermo del Toro's breathing was recorded as part of the Amphibian Man's vocalization.

☐ **Moonlight (2017):** A young African-American man grapples with his identity and sexuality while experiencing the everyday struggles of childhood, adolescence, and burgeoning adulthood. **Memorable Quote:** *"You ain't got to love me, but you gonna know that I love you."*

☐ **Spotlight (2016):** The true story of how the Boston Globe uncovered the massive scandal of child molestation and cover-up within the local Catholic Archdiocese, shaking the entire Catholic Church to its core. **Fun Fact:** All of the journalists use blue pens, their bosses use black pens, and the editor uses a red pen.

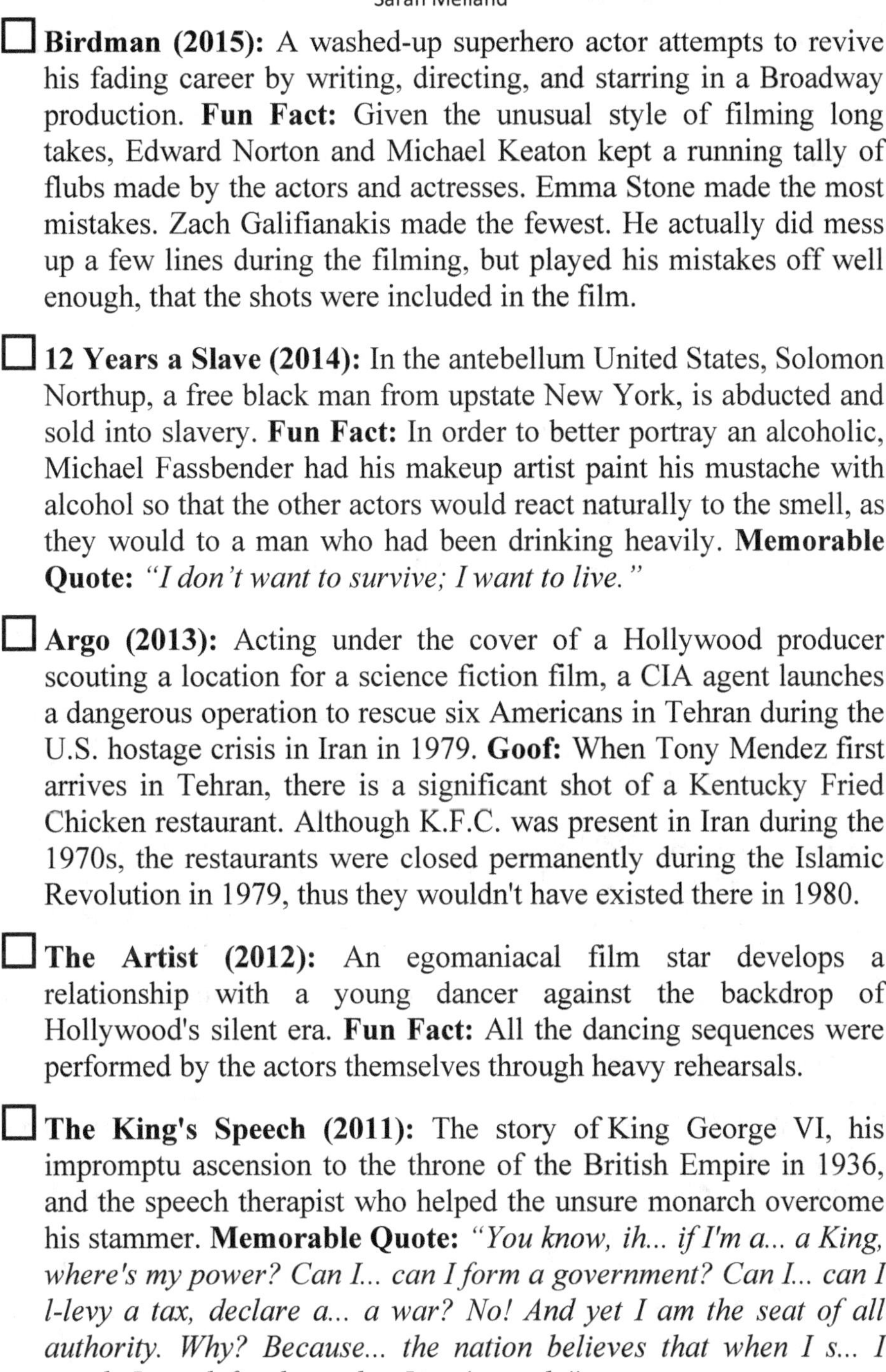

☐ **Birdman (2015):** A washed-up superhero actor attempts to revive his fading career by writing, directing, and starring in a Broadway production. **Fun Fact:** Given the unusual style of filming long takes, Edward Norton and Michael Keaton kept a running tally of flubs made by the actors and actresses. Emma Stone made the most mistakes. Zach Galifianakis made the fewest. He actually did mess up a few lines during the filming, but played his mistakes off well enough, that the shots were included in the film.

☐ **12 Years a Slave (2014):** In the antebellum United States, Solomon Northup, a free black man from upstate New York, is abducted and sold into slavery. **Fun Fact:** In order to better portray an alcoholic, Michael Fassbender had his makeup artist paint his mustache with alcohol so that the other actors would react naturally to the smell, as they would to a man who had been drinking heavily. **Memorable Quote:** *"I don't want to survive; I want to live."*

☐ **Argo (2013):** Acting under the cover of a Hollywood producer scouting a location for a science fiction film, a CIA agent launches a dangerous operation to rescue six Americans in Tehran during the U.S. hostage crisis in Iran in 1979. **Goof:** When Tony Mendez first arrives in Tehran, there is a significant shot of a Kentucky Fried Chicken restaurant. Although K.F.C. was present in Iran during the 1970s, the restaurants were closed permanently during the Islamic Revolution in 1979, thus they wouldn't have existed there in 1980.

☐ **The Artist (2012):** An egomaniacal film star develops a relationship with a young dancer against the backdrop of Hollywood's silent era. **Fun Fact:** All the dancing sequences were performed by the actors themselves through heavy rehearsals.

☐ **The King's Speech (2011):** The story of King George VI, his impromptu ascension to the throne of the British Empire in 1936, and the speech therapist who helped the unsure monarch overcome his stammer. **Memorable Quote:** *"You know, ih... if I'm a... a King, where's my power? Can I... can I form a government? Can I... can I l-levy a tax, declare a... a war? No! And yet I am the seat of all authority. Why? Because... the nation believes that when I s... I speak, I speak for them - but I can't speak."*

☐ **The Hurt Locker (2010):** During the Iraq War, a Sergeant recently assigned to an army bomb squad is put at odds with his squad mates due to his maverick way of handling his work. **Goof:** One character says an Iraqi with a video camera is preparing a clip for YouTube. The scene takes place in 2004. YouTube was created in 2005.

☐ **Slumdog Millionaire (2009):** A Mumbai teenager reflects on his life after being accused of cheating on the Indian version of "Who Wants to be a Millionaire?" **Fun Fact:** Director Danny Boyle placed the money to be paid to the 3 lead child actors in a trust that is to be released to them upon their completion of grade school at 16 years of age. The production company has set up for an auto-rikshaw driver to take the kids to school every day until they are 16 years old.

☐ **No Country for Old Men (2008):** Violence and mayhem ensue after a hunter stumbles upon a drug deal gone wrong and more than two million dollars in cash near the Rio Grande. **Fun Fact:** According to a January 2018 article in Business Insider, a group of psychiatrists studied 400 movies and identified 126 psychopathic characters. They chose Javier Bardem's portrayal of Anton Chigurh as the most clinically accurate portrayal of a psychopath.

☐ **The Departed (2007):** An undercover cop and a mole in the police attempt to identify each other while infiltrating an Irish gang in South Boston. **Best song:** "Shipping Out to Boston." **Fun Fact:** Jack Nicholson pulled a real gun on Leo DiCaprio in The Departed, even though it wasn't in the script. He thought the scene wasn't intense enough before. **My Favorite Line:** *"Maybe. Maybe not. Maybe fuck yourself."*

☐ **Crash (2006):** Los Angeles citizens with vastly separate lives collide in interweaving stories of race, loss and redemption. **Memorable Quote:** *"It's the sense of touch. In any real city, you walk, you know? You brush past people; people bump into you. In L.A., nobody touches you. We're always behind this metal and glass. I think we miss that touch so much, that we crash into each other, just so we can feel something."*

☐ **Million Dollar Baby (2005):** A determined woman works with a hardened boxing trainer to become a professional. **Fun Fact:** Hilary

Swank contracted a bacterial infection from a blister she developed on her foot during training for her role. The infection was so serious that she almost had to be hospitalized for three weeks. Catching the infection in the nick of time, she instead chose to take a week off for medicated rest and didn't tell Clint Eastwood or the other producers of the film about the injury, because she didn't believe it was in character.

- ☐ **The Lord of the Rings: The Return of the King (2004):** Gandalf and Aragorn lead the World of Men against Sauron's army to draw his gaze from Frodo and Sam as they approach Mount Doom with the One Ring. **Goof:** This film features a truly epic battle scene that required a slew of camera angles and tons of coordination. Because of all the complex camerawork, a number of the film's crew members can be spotted lurking within the orc army. Look for the people who aren't dressed to the nines in battle gear, and who don't resemble evil creatures.

- ☐ **Chicago (2003):** Two death-row murderesses develop a fierce rivalry while competing for publicity, celebrity, and a sleazy lawyer's attention. **Best Song: "**Cell Block Tango."

- ☐ **A Beautiful Mind (2002):** After John Nash, a brilliant but asocial mathematician, accepts secret work in cryptography, his life takes a turn for the nightmarish. **Fun Fact:** The equations seen on the classroom chalk boards are actual equations written by the real-life John Nash.

- ☐ **Gladiator (2001):** A former Roman General sets out to exact vengeance against the corrupt emperor who murdered his family and sent him into slavery. **Memorable Quote:** *"Nothing happens to anyone that he is not fitted by nature to bear."*

- ☐ **American Beauty (2000):** A sexually frustrated suburban father has a mid-life crisis after becoming infatuated with his daughter's best friend. **Fun Fact:** The iconic body and hand in the poster for *American Beauty* belong to actress/model Chloe Hunter, not Mena Suvari.

- ☐ **Shakespeare in Love (1999):** The world's greatest ever playwright William Shakespeare, is young, out of ideas and short of cash, but meets his ideal woman and is inspired to write one of his most famous plays. **Fun Fact:** Dame Judi Dench was so taken with the full-sized replica set of the Rose Theater that Miramax gave it to her to take home when filming ended. *Variety* reported in early 1999 that she was looking for a site, and a financial backer, so it could be used as a working theater.

☐ **Titanic (1998):** A seventeen-year-old aristocrat falls in love with a kind but poor artist aboard the luxurious, ill-fated R.M.S. Titanic. **Misquote:** "I'm king of the world!" **Actual Quote:** "I'm *the* king of the world!" **Fun Fact:** The scenes set in 1912, i.e., the whole movie except the present-day scenes and the opening and ending credits, have a total length of two hours and forty minutes, the exact time it took for Titanic to sink. Also, the collision with the iceberg reportedly lasted 37 seconds, which is how long the collision scene is in the movie. **Fun Fact:** Enya was James Cameron's first choice to compose the music for *Titanic.*

☐ **The English Patient (1997):** At the close of World War II, a young nurse tends to a badly-burned plane crash victim. His past is shown in flashbacks, revealing an involvement in a fateful love affair. **Goof:** Katharine Clifton (Scott-Thomas) explains to Count László Almásy (Fiennes), that her husband is map making in Ethiopia. The year at this point is 1939, and the country was known as Abyssinia until 1945.

☐ **Braveheart (1996):** Scottish warrior William Wallace leads his countrymen in a rebellion to free his homeland from the tyranny of King Edward I of England. **Memorable Quote:** *"They may take our lives, but they'll never take our freedom!"*

☐ **Forrest Gump (1995):** The presidencies of Kennedy and Johnson, the Vietnam War, the Watergate scandal and other historical events unfold from the perspective of an Alabama man with an IQ of 75, whose only desire is to be reunited with his childhood sweetheart. **Misquote:** "Mama always said, 'Life is like a box of chocolates.'" **Actual Quote:** "Mama always said life *was* like a box of chocolates." **Memorable Quote:** *"Mama says, 'Stupid is as stupid does'."*

☐ **Schindler's List (1994):** In German-occupied Poland during World War II, industrialist Oskar Schindler gradually becomes concerned for his Jewish workforce after witnessing their persecution by the Nazis. **Fun Fact:** To gather costumes for 20,000 extras, the costume designer took out advertisements seeking clothes. As economic conditions were poor in Poland, many people were eager to sell clothing they still owned from the 1930s and '40s. **Fun Fact:** During production, the atmosphere was so grim and depressing that Steven Spielberg asked his friend Robin Williams if he could tell some jokes and do comedy sketches while Spielberg would watch episodes of *Seinfeld* (1989). Some of Williams' sketches, while played through the speaker phone to the cast and crew, ended up being part of dialogue material for his character in *Aladdin* (1992), the Genie. **Goof:** Steven Spielberg was striving for authenticity when crafting this award-winning drama, but he should've brushed up on his German before filming certain scenes. As an SS soldier drags a boy to an assembly area, he mispronounces the verb "schiessen," which means "to shoot." Instead, he says the verb that means "to defecate."

☐ **Unforgiven (1993):** Retired Old West gunslinger William Munny reluctantly takes on one last job, with the help of his old partner Ned Logan and a young man, The "Schofield Kid." **Memorable Quote:** *"Funny thing, killin' a man. You take away everything he's got and everything he's gonna have."*

☐ **The Silence of the Lambs (1992):** A young F.B.I. cadet must receive the help of an incarcerated and manipulative cannibal killer to help catch another serial killer, a madman who skins his victims. **Misquote:** "Hello, Clarice." **Actual Quote:** "*Good evening,* Clarice." **Fun Fact:** Gene Hackman was originally supposed to play Hannibal. **Memorable Quote:** *"I'm having an old friend for dinner."*

☐ **Dances With Wolves (1991):** Lieutenant John Dunbar, assigned to a remote western Civil War outpost, befriends wolves and Indians, making him an intolerable aberration in the military. **Fun Fact:** During the scene where the buffalo is charging at Smiles a Lot, the buffalo is actually charging at a pile of its favorite treat: Oreo cookies.

☐ **Driving Miss Daisy (1990):** An old Jewish woman and her African-American chauffeur in the American South have a relationship that grows and improves over the years. **Fun Fact:** For all you writers out there, this project was rejected by Walt Disney Studios, 20th Century Fox, Universal, Paramount and Columbia. Basically, don't give up on your dreams when you hear your first no. Cliché, but, whateves.

☐ **Rain Man (1989):** Selfish yuppie Charlie Babbitt's father left a fortune to his savant brother Raymond and a pittance to Charlie; they travel cross-country. **Memorable Quote:** *"I'm an excellent driver."*

☐ **The Last Emperor (1988):** The story of the final Emperor of China. **Fun Fact:** This was the first Western film made in and about the country to be produced with full Chinese government cooperation since 1949.

☐ **Platoon (1987):** Chris Taylor, a neophyte recruit in Vietnam, finds himself caught in a battle of wills between two sergeants, one good and the other evil. A shrewd examination of the brutality of war and the duality of man in conflict. **Memorable Quote: "***Excuses are like assholes, Taylor, everybody got one."*

☐ **Out of Africa (1986):** In 20th-century colonial Kenya, a Danish baroness/plantation owner has a passionate love affair with a free-spirited big-game hunter. **Goof:** Karen offers the tribal chief a box of cigars made by the La Paz factory, in the Netherlands. That factory started exporting cigars in the 1960s.

☐ **Amadeus (1985**): The life, success and troubles of Wolfgang Amadeus Mozart, as told by Antonio Salieri, the contemporaneous composer who was insanely jealous of Mozart's talent and claimed to have murdered him. **Fun Fact:** The film ironically helped spark a revival of Salieri's music, which had previously languished in obscurity.

☐ **Terms of Endearment (1984):** The film follows hard-to-please Aurora looking for love, and her daughter's family problems. **My Favorite Line:** *"If you wanted to get me on my back, all you had to do was ask me."*

☐ **Gandhi (1983):** The life of the lawyer who became the famed leader of the Indian revolts against the British rule through his philosophy of nonviolent protest. **Fun Fact:** The Indian government provided one third of this movie's budget.

☐ **Chariots of Fire (1982):** Two British track athletes, one a determined Jew, and the other a devout Christian, compete in the 1924 Olympics. **Memorable Quote:** *"If I can't win, I won't run!" "If you don't run, you can't win."*

☐ **Ordinary People (1981):** The accidental death of the older son of an affluent family deeply strains the relationships among the bitter mother, the good-natured father, and the guilt-ridden younger son. **Memorable Quote:** *"Well, don't admire people too much. They'll disappoint you sometimes."*

☐ **Kramer vs. Kramer (1980):** Ted Kramer's wife leaves him, allowing for a lost bond to be rediscovered between Ted and his son, Billy. But a heated custody battle ensues over the divorced couple's son, deepening the wounds left by the separation. **Fun Fact:** Dustin Hoffman planned the moment when he throws his wine glass against the wall during the restaurant scene with Meryl Streep. The only person he warned in advance was the cameraman, to make sure that it got in the shot. Streep's shocked reaction was real. In the documentary on the DVD, she recalls yelling at Hoffman as soon as the shot was over for scaring her so badly.

☐ **The Deer Hunter (1979):** An in-depth examination of the ways in which the U.S. Vietnam War impacts and disrupts the lives of people in a small industrial town in Pennsylvania. **Fun Fact:** Co-writer and director Michael Cimino convinced Christopher Walken to spit in Robert De Niro's face. When Walken actually did it, De Niro was completely shocked, as evidenced by his reaction. In fact, De Niro was so furious about it, he nearly left the set. Cimino later said of Walken, "He's got courage!"

☐ **Annie Hall (1978):** Neurotic New York comedian Alvy Singer falls in love with the ditzy Annie Hall. **Memorable Quote:** *"A relationship, I think, is like a shark. You know? It has to constantly move forward or it dies. And I think what we got on our hands is a dead shark."*

☐ **Rocky (1977):** A small-time boxer gets a supremely rare chance to fight a heavy-weight champion in a bout in which he strives to go the distance for his self-respect. **Best Song:** "Eye of the Tiger." **Memorable Quote:** *"Yo, Adrian!"*

☐ **One Flew over the Cuckoo's Nest (1976):** A criminal pleads insanity and is admitted to a mental institution, where he rebels against the oppressive nurse and rallies up the scared patients. **Fun Fact:** Many extras were authentic mental patients.

☐ **The Godfather Part II (1975):** The early life and career of Vito Corleone in 1920s New York City is portrayed, while his son, Michael, expands and tightens his grip on the family crime syndicate. **Goof:** Director Francis Ford Coppola made an intentional cameo in "Apocalypse Now," but his appearance in "The Godfather: Part II" was purely accidental. As young Vito Corleone drives down the street, Coppola's reflection briefly appears in a car window. **Memorable Quote:** *"Keep your friends close, but your enemies closer."*

☐ **The Sting (1974):** Two grifters team up to pull off the ultimate con. **Fun Fact:** Jack Nicholson turned down the role of Johnny Hooker before Robert Redford changed his mind and decided to play it.

☐ **The Godfather (1973):** The aging patriarch of an organized crime dynasty transfers control of his clandestine empire to his reluctant son. **Fun Fact:** Marlon Brando wanted to make Don Corleone "look like a bulldog," so he stuffed his cheeks with cotton wool for the audition. For the actual filming, he wore a mouthpiece made by a dentist. This appliance is on display in the American Museum of the Moving Image in Queens, New York. **Fun Facts:** The cat held by Marlon Brando in the opening scene was a stray that Coppola found while on the lot at Paramount, and was not originally called for in the script. So content was the cat that its purring muffled some of Brando's dialogue, and, as a result, most of his lines had to be looped. **Fun Fact:** During an early shot of the scene where Vito Corleone returns home and his people carry him up the stairs, Marlon Brando put weights under his body on the bed as a prank, to make it harder to lift him. **Fun Fact:** James Caan improvised the, now immortal, phrase "Bada-Bing" on the set of *The Godfather*.

Goof: The most egregious error in Francis Ford Coppola's 1972 masterpiece comes when Sonny attacks Carlo outside some apartment buildings. In the midst of the beating, Sonny throws a whiff that can be spotted from a mile away, though it's portrayed as a direct hit. It might very well be the most famous "movie" punch in cinematic history. **Memorable Quote:** *"I'm going to make him an offer he can't refuse."*

☐ **The French Connection (1972):** A pair of NYC cops in the Narcotics Bureau stumble onto a drug smuggling job with a French connection. **Goof:** As the train is speeding down the track Pierre Nicoli is holding a gun to the motorman's head. The safety on the gun is engaged and it cannot shoot.

☐ **Patton (1971):** The World War II phase of the career of controversial American general George S. Patton. **Goof:** Patton is shown having read a book, "The Tank in Attack", by his adversary, Erwin Rommel. The book *Panzer Greift An* was however never finished by Rommel. Most of what was to be in "The Tank in Attack" can be found in the book "The Rommel Papers", which is made from notes and diary entries by Field Marshal Rommel during the Africa campaign.

☐ **Midnight Cowboy (1970):** A naive hustler travels from Texas to New York City to seek personal fortune, finding a new friend in the process. **Memorable Quote:** *"I'm walking here! I'm walking here!"*

☐ **Oliver! (1969):** After being sold to a mortician, young orphan Oliver Twist runs away and meets a group of boys trained to be pickpockets by an elderly mentor. **Memorable Quote:** *"Please sir, I want some more."*

☐ **In the Heat of the Night (1968):** The cases and adventures of the police forces in and around Sparta, Mississippi. **Memorable Quote:** *"They call me Mister Tibbs!"*

☐ **A Man for All Seasons (1967):** The story of Sir Thomas More, who stood up to King Henry VIII when the King rejected the Roman Catholic Church to obtain a divorce and remarry. **Fun Fact:** The trial and execution scenes are based very closely on an eyewitness account, published anonymously in the Paris Newsletter of August 4, 1535.

☐ **The Sound of Music (1966):** A woman leaves an Austrian convent to become a governess to a Naval officer widower's children. **Best Song:** "Do-Re-Mi"

☐ **My Fair Lady (1965):** Snobbish phonetics Professor Henry Higgins agrees to a wager that he can make flower girl Eliza Doolittle presentable in high society. **Fun Fact:** When Audrey Hepburn was first informed that her voice wasn't strong enough and that she would have to be dubbed, she walked out. She returned the next day and, in a typically graceful Hepburn gesture, apologized to everybody for her "wicked behavior."

☐ **Tom Jones (1964):** The romantic and chivalrous adventures of adopted bastard Tom Jones in 18th-century England. **Memorable Quote:** *"It is not true that drink alters a man's character. It may reveal it more fully."*

☐ **Lawrence of Arabia (1963):** The story of T.E. Lawrence, the English officer who successfully united and led the diverse, often warring, Arab tribes during World War I in order to fight the Turks. **Goof:** Based on the life of T.E. Lawrence, a British officer stationed in the Middle East during WWI, "Lawrence of Arabia" takes plenty of liberty with the actual facts of its hero's story. It also takes plenty of liberty with Bedouin traditions, as demonstrated by one scene where Lawrence uses his left hand to eat food offered by his Bedu guide. This would have been a major taboo, as the left hand was used to clean oneself after using the bathroom and the right was used to eat.

☐ **West Side Story (1962):** Two youngsters from rival New York City gangs fall in love, but tensions between their respective friends build toward tragedy. **Fun Facts:** The actors in the rival gangs were instructed to play pranks on each other off the set to keep tensions high.

☐ **The Apartment (1961):** A man tries to rise in his company by letting its executives use his apartment for trysts, but complications and a romance of his own ensue. **Memorable Quote:** *"Ya know, I* *used to live like Robinson Crusoe; I mean, shipwrecked among eight million people. And then one day I saw a footprint in the sand, and there you were."*

☐ **Ben-Hur (1960):** After a Jewish prince is betrayed and sent into slavery by a Roman friend, he regains his freedom and comes back for revenge. **Goof:** Sheik Ilderim pins a Star of David onto Ben-Hur's belt before the race, obviously to goad the Romans. The Star of David didn't become a symbol of Judaism until the Middle Ages, in Eastern Europe. The first reference occurs in the 12th Century.

☐ **Gigi (1959):** Weary of the conventions of Parisian society, a rich playboy and a youthful courtesan-in-training enjoy a platonic friendship which may not stay platonic for long. **Fun Fact:** The entire film was written, cast and ready to shoot in four and a half months.

☐ **The Bridge on the River Kwai (1958):** British POWs are forced to build a railway bridge across the river Kwai for their Japanese captors, not knowing that the allied forces are planning to destroy it. **Goof:** Japan was not a signatory of the Geneva Conventions until 1953, therefore there was no expectation by Allied prisoners of being treated in accordance with them. In fact, the Japanese treatment of prisoners led to the review and update of the conventions in 1949.

☐ **Around the World in 80 Days (1957):** A Victorian Englishman bets that with the new steamships and railways he can circumnavigate the globe in eighty days. **Fun Fact:** This movie created the idea of "cameo roles" as a way to invite established stars to participate in a production.

☐ **Marty (1956):** A middle-aged butcher and a school teacher who have given up on the idea of love meet at a dance and fall for each other. **Fun Fact:** Betsy Blair, who portrayed Clara, was almost not permitted to do the film by Hecht-Lancaster Productions and United Artists due to the 1950s Hollywood Blacklist. However, Gene Kelly, her husband at the time, basically blackmailed United Artists and Hecht-Lancaster into casting her, at the last minute, by threatening not to direct or star in any of UA's or Hecht Lancaster's productions if she was not cast for the role.

☐ **On the Waterfront (1955):** An ex-prize fighter turned longshoreman struggles to stand up to his corrupt union bosses. **Memorable Quote:** *"You don't understand! I coulda had class. I coulda been a contender. I could've been somebody, instead of a bum, which is what I am."*

☐ **From Here to Eternity (1954):** In Hawaii in 1941, a private is cruelly punished for not boxing on his unit's team, while his captain's wife and second-in-command are falling in love. **Memorable Quote:** *"Nobody ever lies about being lonely."*

☐ **The Greatest Show on Earth (1953):** The dramatic lives of trapeze artists, a clown, and an elephant trainer are told against a background of circus spectacle. **Fun Fact:** It took one hour for Cecil B De Mille and Charlton Heston to find the right hat which Heston had to wear. De Mille said that audiences took more attention to the hat than to the shoes.

☐ **An American in Paris (1952):** Three friends struggle to find work in Paris. Things become more complicated when two of them fall in love with the same woman. **Fun Fact:** No words are spoken during the last 20 minutes and 25 seconds of the film. **Memorable Quote:** *"Back home everyone said I didn't have any talent. They might be saying the same thing over here but it sounds better in French."*

☐ **All About Eve (1951):** An ingénue insinuates herself into the lives of an established but aging stage actress and her circle of theater friends. **Misquote:** "Fasten your seat belts, it's going to be a bumpy ride." **Actual:** "Fasten your seat belts, it's going to be a bumpy *night."* **Goof:** This timeless drama deals with the ins and outs of show business, so it's almost meta when Addison slaps Eve and her head turns the wrong way. Actress Anne Baxter's minor blunder is otherwise known as a "stage" slap.

☐ **All the Kings Men (1950):** The rise and fall of a corrupt politician, who makes his friends richer and retains power by dint of a populist appeal. **Memorable Quote:** *"Appeal to their emotions. Make them laugh; make them cry; make them mad, even if they get mad at you. But for heaven's sake, don't try to improve their minds."*

☐ **Hamlet (1949):** Prince Hamlet struggles over whether or not he should kill his uncle, whom he suspects has murdered his father, the former king. **Memorable Quote:** *"To be, or not to be: that is the question."*

☐ **Gentleman's Agreement (1948):** A reporter pretends to be Jewish in order to cover a story on anti-Semitism, and personally discovers the true depths of bigotry and hatred. **Fun Fact:** Celeste Holm is on record as saying that she found Gregory Peck to be no fun to work with.

☐ **The Best Years of Our Lives (1947):** Three World War II veterans return home to small-town America to discover that they and their families have been irreparably changed. **Fun Fact:** To avoid awkwardness when he first met his fellow cast members, Harold Russell made a point of reaching out with his hooks and taking their hands, thus putting them at ease with his disability.

☐ **The Lost Weekend (1946):** The desperate life of a chronic alcoholic is followed through a four-day drinking bout. **Fun Fact:** Ray Milland actually checked himself into Bellevue Hospital with the help of resident doctors, in order to experience the horror of a drunk ward. Milland was given an iron bed and locked inside the "booze tank." That night, a new arrival came into the ward screaming, an entrance that immersed the whole ward in hysteria. With the ward falling into bedlam, a robed and barefoot Milland escaped while the door was ajar and slipped out onto 34th Street where he tried to hail a cab. A suspicious cop spotted him, Milland tried to explain, but the cop didn't believe him, especially after he noticed the Bellevue insignia on his robe. The actor was dragged back to Bellevue where it took him a half-hour to explain his situation to the authorities before he was finally released.

☐ **Going My Way (1945):** When young Father O'Malley arrives at St. Dominic's, old Father Fitzgibbon doesn't think much of the church's newest member. **Goof:** it was common custom at the time for opera singers to be classified as either soprano or contralto (alto). The term mezzo-soprano only gradually became more widespread from the 50s onwards. Now, of course, she is more correctly known as a mezzo-soprano, but in the 40s she would have been referred to as a contralto.

☐ **Casablanca (1944):** A cynical American expatriate struggles to decide whether or not he should help his former lover and her fugitive husband escape French Morocco. **Misquote:** "Play it *again*, Sam" **Actual quote:** "Play it, Sam. Play 'As Time Goes By'." **Fun Fact:** Sam was actually a drummer. **Fun Fact:** Ronald Reagan was originally announced as the lead for *Casablanca.* The proclamation turned out to simply be a ruse to keep the actor's name in the press. **Goof:** Inside Rick Blaine's Moroccan night club, a now-famous piano player named Sam sets the atmosphere. Only Wilson didn't actually know how to play the piano. It's no wonder, then, that his hand movements don't match the music whatsoever. **Memorable Quote:** *"Here's looking at you, kid."* **Memorable Quote:** *"Louis, I think this is the beginning of a beautiful friendship."* **Memorable Quote:** *"We'll always have Paris."* **My Favorite Line:** *"Of all the gin joints in all the towns in all the world, she walks into mine."*

☐ **Mrs. Miniver (1943):** A British family struggles to survive the first months of World War II. **Fun Fact:** In real life, shortly after shooting was completed, Greer Garson married Richard Ney, who plays her son, Vin, in the film.

☐ **How Green Was My Valley (1942):** At the turn of the century in a Welsh mining village, the Morgans raise coal-mining sons and hope their youngest will find a better life. **Fun Fact:** *How Green Was My Valley* famously beat Orson Welles' *Citizen Kane* (1941) to a Best Picture Oscar.

☐ **Rebecca (1941):** A self-conscious woman juggles adjusting to her new role as an aristocrat's wife and avoiding being intimidated by his first wife's spectral presence. **Memorable Quote:** *"I'm asking you to marry me, you little fool."*

☐ **Gone with the Wind (1940):** A manipulative woman and a roguish man conduct a turbulent romance during the American Civil War and Reconstruction periods. **Goof:** The film takes place before the invention of the lightbulb, yet a number of lamps in the film have either a cord or bulb. **My Favorite Line:** *"Frankly, my dear, I don't* *give a damn." **Memorable Quote:** "As God is my witness, I'll never be hungry again." **Memorable Quote:** "After all, tomorrow is another day."*

☐ **You Can't Take It with You (1939):** A man from a family of rich snobs becomes engaged to a woman from a good-natured but decidedly eccentric family. **Fun Fact:** Shortly before filming began, Lionel Barrymore lost the use of his legs to crippling arthritis and a hip injury. To accommodate him, the script was altered so that his character had a sprained ankle, and Barrymore did the film on crutches.

☐ **The Life of Emile Zola (1938):** The biopic of the famous French muckraking writer and his involvement in fighting the injustice of the Dreyfuss Affair. **Fun Fact:** This was the first film to break double digits in Academy Award nominations, receiving an astonishing ten nods.

☐ **The Great Ziegfeld (1937):** The ups and downs of Florenz Ziegfeld Jr., famed producer of extravagant stage revues, are portrayed. **Goof:** Ziegfeld is depicted as dying in New York City. He actually died of lung disease in Hollywood, California, a few days after moving there from a specialty hospital in New Mexico.

☐ **Mutiny on the Bounty (1936):** First mate Fletcher Christian leads a revolt against his sadistic commander, Captain Bligh, in this classic seafaring adventure, based on the real-life 1788 mutiny. **Fun Fact:** Not only did Marlon Brando improvise his lines in scenes with Trevor Howard, making it impossible for his co-star to pick up his cues, but he even started putting cotton in his ears so he couldn't hear Howard's lines. I think Marlon Brando just really likes cotton balls (See Fun Fact for "The Godfather.")

☐ **It Happened One Night (1935):** A renegade reporter and a crazy young heiress meet on a bus heading for New York, and end up stuck with each other when the bus leaves them behind at one of the stops. **Memorable Quote:** *"Well shut my big nasty mouth!"*

☐ **Cavalcade (1933/1934):** A portrayal of the triumphs and tragedies of two English families, the upper-crust Marryots and the working-class Bridgeses, from 1899 to 1933. **Memorable Quote:** *"There* *should never be any good reason for neglecting someone that you love."*

☐ **Grand Hotel (1932/1933):** A group of very different individuals staying at a luxurious hotel in Berlin deal with each of their respective dramas. **Fun Fact:** There should never be any good reason for neglecting someone that you love.

☐ **Cimarron (1931/1932):** newspaper editor settles in an Oklahoma boom town with his reluctant wife at the end of the nineteenth century. **Goof:** During the period of the film set in 1907, Yancey is the Progressive Party's candidate for governor of Oklahoma. The Progressive Party did not form until 1912, and then disbanded after Theodore Roosevelt's unsuccessful third-party candidacy that year.

☐ **All Quiet on the Western Front (1930/1931):** A German youth eagerly enters World War I, but his enthusiasm wanes as he gets a firsthand view of the horror. **Fun Fact:** Lewis Milestone deliberately made the film without music so as not to take away from the seriousness of the subject. Much to his chagrin, however, some movie theaters added music in of their own choosing, as they weren't used to having films delivered to them without any form of background scoring.

☐ **The Broadway Melody (1929/1930):** A pair of sisters from the vaudeville circuit try to make it big time on Broadway, but matters of the heart complicate the attempt. **Fun Fact:** A silent version was also released, as many cinemas hadn't yet acquired sound equipment in 1929.

☐ **Wings (1928/1929):** Two young men, one rich, one middle class, who are in love with the same woman, become fighter pilots in World War I. **Fun Fact:** This film marks the first time that actors were filmed flying in the air.

Academy Awards

Best Original Screenplay

I included these in my list as I am a screenwriter and love watching how people construct their films. Obviously, if they won Best Movie and Best Original screenplay, I only included it in the first list, that's why there might be missing years.

- ☐ **Promising Young Woman (2020):** A young woman, traumatized by a tragic event in her past, seeks out vengeance against those who crossed her path. **Fun Fact:** The title is likely a reference to Brock Turner, a Stanford University student, who was convicted of sexual assault in 2016. The judge sentenced him to only six months in prison on the basis that he was a "promising young man."
- ☐ **Get Out (2017):** A young African-American visits his white girlfriend's parents for the weekend, where his simmering uneasiness about their reception of him eventually reaches a boiling point. **Fun Fact:** Daniel Kaluuya was given the lead role on the spot after nailing his audition. Jordan Peele said Kaluuya did about five takes of a key scene, in which his character needs to cry, and each was so perfect that the single tear came down at the exact same time for each take.
- ☐ **Manchester by the Sea (2016):** A depressed uncle is asked to take care of his teenage nephew after the boy's father dies. **Goof:** Lee is shown purchasing beer in a convenience store at 2 AM. In Massachusetts it is illegal for a store to sell beer after 11 PM.
- ☐ **Her (2013):** In a near future, a lonely writer develops an unlikely relationship with an operating system designed to meet his every need.

☐ **Django Unchained (2012):** With the help of a German bounty-hunter, a freed slave sets out to rescue his wife from a brutal plantation-owner in Mississippi. **Fun Fact:** When Calvin Candie (Leonardo DiCaprio) smashes his hand on the dinner table, DiCaprio accidentally crushed a small stemmed glass with his palm and really began to bleed. He ignored it, stayed in character, and continued with the scene. Quentin Tarantino was so impressed that he used this take in the final print, and when he called cut, the room erupted in a standing ovation.

☐ **Midnight in Paris (2011):** While on a trip to Paris with his fiancée's family, a nostalgic screenwriter finds himself mysteriously going back to the 1920s every day at midnight. **Memorable Quote:** *"We all fear death and question our place in the universe. The artist's job is not to succumb to despair, but to find an antidote for the emptiness of existence."*

☐ **Milk (2008):** The story of Harvey Milk and his struggles as an American gay activist who fought for gay rights and became California's first openly gay elected official. **Goof:** The date of the election in which Harvey Milk was elected Supervisor is shown on the screen as November 7, 1977. It is customary for such elections to be held on the Tuesday immediately following the first Monday in November. In 1977, November 7 fell on the first Monday, so the election would have been held on November 8, not November 7.

☐ **Juno (2007):** Faced with an unplanned pregnancy, an offbeat young woman makes an unusual decision regarding the unborn child.

☐ **Little Mis Sunshine (2006):** A family determined to get their young daughter into the finals of a beauty pageant take a cross-country trip in their VW bus. **Fun Fact:** The production crew made sure Abigail Breslin really was listening to music in her headphones to keep her from hearing Alan Arkin's profanity-laced scenes.

☐ **Eternal Sunshine of the Spotless Mind (2004):** When their relationship turns sour, a couple undergoes a medical procedure to have each other erased from their memories. **Memorable Quote:** *"Constantly talking isn't necessarily communicating."*

☐ **Lost in Translation (2003):** A faded movie star and a neglected young woman form an unlikely bond after crossing paths in Tokyo. **Goof:** At 47:28, when Bob and Charlotte get in the taxi, you can see Bob closing the rear door. This is a mistake, since in Japan taxi's doors are operated exclusively by the driver. Passengers do not open nor close them.

☐ **Talk to Her (2002):** Two men share an odd friendship while they care for two women who are both in deep comas.

☐ **Gosford Park (2001):** Set in the 1930s, this movie brings a group of pretentious rich and famous together for a weekend of relaxation at a hunting resort. But when a murder occurs, each one of these interesting characters becomes a suspect. **Goof:** The movie takes place in 1932 but some of the songs Ivor Novello sings for the guests didn't come out until years after, like "Glamorous Night" (1935), "Why It Wasn't You" (1937), "I Can Give You a Starlight" (1939) and "Waltz of My Heart" (1939).

☐ **Almost Famous (2000):** A high-school boy is given the chance to write a story for Rolling Stone Magazine about an up-and-coming rock band as he accompanies them on their concert tour. **Fun Fact:** In order to credibly portray a rock band, the members of Stillwater in *Almost Famous* rehearsed for four hours a night, five nights a week, for six weeks.

☐ **Good Will Hunting (1997):** Will Hunting, a janitor at M.I.T., has a gift for mathematics, but needs help from a psychologist to find direction in his life. **My Favorite Line:** *"How'd ya like them apples?"*

☐ **Fargo (1996):** Jerry Lundegaard's inept crime falls apart due to his and his henchmen's bungling and the persistent police work of the quite pregnant Marge Gunderson.

☐ **The Usual Suspects (1995):** A sole survivor tells of the twisty events leading up to a horrific gun battle on a boat, which began when five criminals met at a seemingly random police lineup. **Fun Fact:** The idea for the poster for *The Usual Suspects* came before any script or story. **Fun Fact:** The childish snickering during *The Usual Suspects* iconic line-up was genuine, caused by Benicio Del Toro's persistent flatulence. **Memorable Quotes:** *"The greatest trick the devil ever pulled was convincing the world he didn't exist."*

☐ **Pulp Fiction (1994):** The lives of two mob hitmen, a boxer, a gangster and his wife, and a pair of diner bandits intertwine in four tales of violence and redemption. **Fun Fact:** The shot of Vincent plunging the syringe into Mia's chest was filmed by having John Travolta pull the needle out, then running the film backwards. Watch carefully and you'll see a mark on Mia's chest disappear when she's revived. **Goof:** In one of this film's best scenes, a young man emerges from the bathroom and lets the bullets fly toward Vincent and Jules. Before that bathroom door even opens, however, at least two bullet holes are already in the wall.

☐ **The Crying Game (1992):** A British soldier kidnapped by IRA terrorists soon befriends one of his captors, who then becomes drawn into the soldier's world.

☐ **Thelma and Louise (1991):** Two best friends set out on an adventure, but it soon turns into a terrifying escape from the police. **Fun Fact:** It took producers so long to find someone for the role of Louise that Geena Davis had to sign a contract stating that the producers could cast her in either role if need be.

☐ **Ghost (1990):** After a young man is murdered, his spirit stays behind to warn his lover of impending danger, with the help of a reluctant psychic.

☐ **Dead Poets Society (1989):** Maverick teacher John Keating uses poetry to embolden his boarding school students to new heights of self-expression. **Memorable Quote:** *"Carpe diem. Seize the day, boys. Make your lives extraordinary."*

☐ **Moonstruck (1987):** Loretta Castorini, a bookkeeper from Brooklyn, New York, finds herself in a difficult situation when she falls for the brother of the man she has agreed to marry. **Memorable Quote:** *"Snap out of it!"*

☐ **Hannah and Her Sisters (1986):** Between two Thanksgivings two years apart, Hannah's husband falls in love with her sister Lee, while her hypochondriac ex-husband rekindles his relationship with her sister Holly.

☐ **Witness (1985):** When a young Amish boy is sole witness to a murder, policeman John Book goes into hiding in Amish country to protect him until the trial. **Goof:** The Amish clothes are shown with buttons, namely on men's shirts and coats. The Amish use straight pins in place of buttons, whereas Mennonites use buttons on their clothes.

☐ **Places in the Heart (1984):** In central Texas in the 1930s, a widow, with two small children, tries to run her small 40-acre farm with the help of two disparate people.

☐ **Tender Mercies (1983):** A broken-down, middle-aged country singer gets a new wife, reaches out to his long-lost daughter, and tries to put his troubled life back together. **Fun Fact:** Robert Duvall is really singing in the nightclub scene.

☐ **Melvin and Howard (1980):** The story of hard-luck Melvin E. Dummar, who claimed to have received a will naming him an heir to the fortune of Howard Hughes.

☐ **Breaking away (1979):** A small-town boy obsessed with the Italian cycling team vies for the affections of a college girl. **Fun Fact:** Shot during the spring of 1978 during spring break. Indiana University had a three-week spring break due to a coal strike. Coal was used to heat the entire university.

☐ **Coming Home (1978):** A woman whose husband is fighting in Vietnam falls in love with another man who suffered a paralyzing combat injury there.

☐ **Network (1976):** A television network cynically exploits a deranged former anchor's ravings and revelations about the news media for its own profit. **My Favorite Line:** *"I'm mad as hell, and I'm not going to take this anymore!"*

☐ **Dog Day Afternoon (1975):** Three amateur bank robbers plan to hold up a bank. A nice simple robbery: Walk in, take the money, and run. Unfortunately, the supposedly uncomplicated heist suddenly becomes a bizarre nightmare as everything that could go wrong does.

☐ **Chinatown (1974):** A private detective hired to expose an adulterer finds himself caught up in a web of deceit, corruption and murder. **Fun Fact:** When filming *Chinatown* Jack Nicholson was dating Anjelica Huston, the daughter of his screen nemesis John Huston. She visited the set on the day that her father's character asked Nicolson's Jake Gittes, "Did you sleep with my daughter?" **Memorable Quote:** *"Forget it, Jake, it's Chinatown."*

☐ **The Candidate (1972):** Bill McKay is a candidate for the U.S. Senate from California. He has no hope of winning, so he is willing to tweak the establishment.

☐ **The Hospital (1971):** A hospital's chief-of-staff struggles to find meaning in his life during a spate of staff deaths.

☐ **Butch Cassidy and the Sundance Kid (1969):** Wyoming, early 1900s. Butch Cassidy and The Sundance Kid are the leaders of a band of outlaws. After a train robbery goes wrong, they find themselves on the run with a posse hard on their heels. Their solution - escape to Bolivia. **Fun Fact:** The original title was the other way around.

☐ **The Producers (1967):** A stage-play producer devises a plan to make money by producing a sure-fire flop. **Fun Fact:** Gene Wilder said in an interview on TCM that at the first reading of the script, he excused himself to leave for a dentist appointment he could not miss, when in fact he had to go to the unemployment office to collect a check for $55 he desperately needed at the time.

- ☐ **Guess Who's Coming to Dinner (1967):** A couple's attitudes are challenged when their daughter introduces them to her African-American fiancé. **Fun Fact (SPOILER):** In the scene near the end where Spencer Tracy gives his memorable soliloquy, Katharine Hepburn can be seen crying in the background. This was not acting: she knew how gravely ill her longtime lover was and was moved by his remarks about how true love endures through the years. **Also:** Spencer Tracy and Katharine Hepburn kept their more than two-decade long relationship a secret.

- ☐ **A Man and a Woman (1966):** A widow and a widower find their relationship developing into love, but their past tragedies prove hard to overcome, causing them to proceed with utmost delicacy.

- ☐ **Darling (1965):** Beautiful but amoral model Diana Scott sleeps her way to the top of the London fashion scene at the height of the Swinging Sixties. **Memorable Quote:** *"Your idea of fidelity is not having more than one man in a bed at the same time."*

- ☐ **Father Goose (1964):** During World War II, a man persuaded to live on an isolated island and spot aircraft finds himself responsible for a teacher and several students, all female.

- ☐ **How the West was Won (1962):** A family saga covering several decades of Westward expansion in the nineteenth century - including the Gold Rush, the Civil War, and the building of the railroads. **Goof:** When the wagon train, on its way to California, is attacked by Indians, it is in a mountainous area, yet the Indians are identified as Cheyenne. The Cheyenne tribe was a Great Plains tribe, and would not have been that far west.

- ☐ **Divorce Italian Style (1961):** A married Sicilian baron falls in love with his cousin and vows to wed her, but with divorce illegal he must concoct a crime of passion to do away with his wife.

☐ **Splendor in the Grass (1961):** A fragile Kansas girl's love for a handsome young man from the town's most powerful family drives her to heartbreak and madness. **Fun Fact:** The nightclub owner played by Phyllis Diller is Texas Guinan, a real-life New York nightclub owner of the 1920's. "Hello, suckers!" was her standard nightly greeting to her nightclub patrons.

☐ **Pillow Talk (1959):** A man and a woman who share a party line cannot stand each other, but he has fun romancing her with his voice disguised. **Memorable Quote:** *"I've had hangovers before, but this time, even my hair hurts."*

☐ **The Defiant Ones (1958):** Two escaped convicts chained together, white and black, must learn to get along in order to elude capture.

☐ **Designing Woman (1957):** A sportswriter and a fashion-designer marry after a whirlwind romance, and discover they have little in common. **Fun Fact:** James Stewart and Grace Kelly were intended to be the co-stars of this movie, but when Kelly became betrothed to Prince Rainier of Monaco, Stewart decided not to do it (a decision he later said he regretted), and the leading roles went to Gregory Peck and Lauren Bacall.

☐ **The Red Balloon (1956):** A red balloon with a mind of its own follows a little boy around the streets of Paris.

☐ **The Country Girl (1954):** A director hires an alcoholic has-been and strikes up a stormy relationship with the actor's wife, who he believes is the cause of all the man's problems. **Fun Fact:** Grace Kelly won her only Oscar for her role in this movie beating out Judy Garland, the sentimental favorite, in the closest Best Actress race in Academy history besides the Barbra Streisand and Katharine Hepburn tie for 1968. A reported six votes were all that separated the cinematic legends.

☐ **The Bad and the Beautiful (1952):** An unscrupulous movie producer uses an actress, a director and a writer to achieve success.

☐ **A Place in the Sun (1951):** A poor boy gets a job working for his rich uncle and ends up falling in love with two women. **Memorable Quote:** *"Of course. I'm always late. Part of my charm."*

☐ **A Letter to Three Wives (1949):** A letter is addressed to three wives from their "best friend" Addie Ross, announcing that she is running away with one of their husbands - but she does not say which one.

☐ **The Bachelor and the Bobby-Soxer (1947):** A high school girl falls for a playboy artist, with screwball results. **My Two Cents:** Cary Grant is my favorite actor.

☐ **The Seventh Veil (1945):** A concert pianist with amnesia fights to regain her memory. **Fun Fact:** James Mason and Ann Todd had an affair while working on the film

☐ **Marie-Louise (1944):** Amidst the Nazi invasion of France in 1942, a young girl is evacuated to Switzerland but is still haunted by the terrors she has witnessed.

☐ **Wilson (1944):** A chronicle of the political career of US President Woodrow Wilson. **Goof:** When Wilson is elected governor of New Jersey, the movie states that he won all 22 counties. New Jersey has (and had in 1910) only 21 counties.

☐ **Princess O'Rourke (1943):** A pilot falls in love with a woman he believes is heading cross country to become a maid, little suspecting that she's actually a princess.

☐ **Woman of the Year (1942):** Rival reporters Sam and Tess fall in love and get married, only to find their relationship strained when Sam comes to resent Tess' hectic lifestyle. **Fun Fact:** Knowing of Spencer Tracy's reputation as a heavy drinker, Katharine Hepburn served him strong tea between scenes. She also got him to paint, as she did, as an escape from the pressures of Hollywood life.

☐ **Here Comes Mr. Jordan (1941):** Boxer Joe Pendleton dies 50 years too soon due to a heavenly mistake, and is given a new life as a millionaire playboy.

☐ **Arise My Love (1940):** A dashing pilot and a vivacious reporter have romantic and dramatic adventures in Europe as World War II begins. **Fun Fact:** Claudette Colbert once said that this was her favorite of all of her films.

☐ **Mr. Smith Goes to Washington (1939):** A naive man is appointed to fill a vacancy in the United States Senate. His plans promptly collide with political corruption, but he doesn't back down.

☐ **Boys Town (1938):** When a death row prisoner tells him, he wouldn't have led a life of crime if only he had had one friend as a child, Father Edward Flanagan decides to start a home for young boys. **Fun Fact:** When shooting began on the movie Mickey Rooney repeatedly tried to steal scenes by fumbling with a handkerchief, pulling faces and other bits of business. This so annoyed Spencer Tracy that he threatened to have Rooney thrown off the movie unless he behaved.

☐ **A Star is Born (1937):** A Young woman comes to Hollywood with dreams of stardom, and achieves them only with the help of an alcoholic leading man whose best days are behind him.

☐ **The Story of Louis Pasteur (1936):** The biography of the pioneering French microbiologist who helped revolutionize agriculture and medicine. **Goof:** Pasteur refers to the "rabies virus" prior to completing development of his vaccine and immunization of Joseph Meister in 1885, but the idea of a non-bacterial pathogen didn't exist until 1892, and the term "virus" itself was coined when the first (tobacco mosaic) was isolated in 1898.

☐ **The Scoundrel (1935):** A ruthless, cynical, hated publisher is killed in a plane crash, doomed to be a "restless" spirit for being unloved.

A heavenly power gives him a month on Earth to find one person to shed a tear for him before his fate is sealed.

- ☐ **Manhattan Melodrama (1934):** The friendship between two orphans endures even though they grow up on opposite sides of the law and fall in love with the same woman. **Goof:** There is a scene depicting a rabble-rousing speech by Leon Trotsky, which descends into a riot, circa 1904. In reality Trotsky didn't visit the United States until January 13 1917 for a short while before returning to Russia. In 1904, he was active in the events leading up to the 1905 Russian Revolution.

- ☐ **One Way Passage (1932):** A terminally ill woman and a debonair murderer facing execution meet and fall in love on a trans-Pacific crossing, each without knowing the other's secret.

- ☐ **The Champ (1931):** An alcoholic ex-boxer struggles to provide a good living for his son. **Fun Fact:** Wallace Beery actually got one less vote than Fredric March in the 1931/1932 Academy Awards voting for best actor, but the rules at the time considered anyone with one or two votes less than the leader as being in a tie. So, both got Academy Awards.

- ☐ **The Dawn Patrol (1930):** World War I ace Dick Courtney derides the leadership of his superior officer, but Courtney is soon promoted to squadron commander and learns harsh lessons about sending subordinates to their deaths.

- ☐ **The Big House (1930):** A convict falls in love with his new cellmate's sister, only to become embroiled in a planned break-out which is certain to have lethal consequences. **Fun Fact:** Frances Marion's Academy Award for Best Screenplay made her the first woman to win an Oscar in a non-acting capacity.

- ☐ **The Patriot (1928):** Paul I, the Emperor of All Russia, becomes the target of a deadly conspiracy. **Fun Fact:** This film was nominated for a Best Picture Oscar for 1929 and since no complete print of the film seems to have survived, it has the (unfortunate) distinction of being the only film nominated for Best Picture to have been lost. Which is super sad since we won't be able to ever complete this list.

- ☐ **Underworld (1927):** Boisterous gangster kingpin Bull Weed rehabilitates his former lawyer from his alcoholic haze, but complications arise when he falls for Weed's girlfriend.

Action/Adventure

Action and adventure have long been established features of American and other national cinemas. Associated with narratives of quest and discovery, and spectacular scenes of combat, violence and pursuit, action and adventure films are not restricted to any particular historical or geographic setting. Indeed, the basic elements of conflict, chase, and challenge can be inflected in any number of different directions. As such, action and adventure as cinematic forms are constantly in the process of reinvention, manifesting themselves in a multiplicity of different genres and sub-genres over time. It is nonetheless useful to distinguish between the two terms and the kind of cinema to which they refer, since "action," "adventure," and "action-adventure" are all descriptors with difference valences. With this in mind, a rudimentary distinction can be made between action *sequences* and adventure *narratives*. Action is associated with a particular kind of scene or spectacle (explosions, chases, combat); adventure, by contrast, implies a story (typically, though not always, the quest narrative) often located within a fantasy or exoticized setting.

☐ **The Adventures of Robin Hood (1938):** When Prince John and the Norman Lords begin oppressing the Saxon masses in King Richard's absence, a Saxon lord fights back as the outlaw leader of a rebel guerrilla army.

☐ **The African Queen (1951):** In WWI Africa, a gin-swilling riverboat captain is persuaded by a strait-laced missionary to use his boat to attack an enemy warship. **My Two Cents:** Katherine Hepburn might be my favorite actress of all-time, and close second would, obviously, be Meryl Streep.

☐ **Barry Lyndon (1975):** An Irish rogue wins the heart of a rich widow and assumes her dead husband's aristocratic position in 18th-century England.

☐ **Cast Away (2000):** A FedEx executive undergoes a physical and emotional transformation after crash landing on a deserted island. **Fun Fact:** To make himself look like an average out of shape middle aged man Tom Hanks didn't exercise and allowed himself to grow pudgy. Production was then halted for a year so he could lose fifty pounds and grow out his hair for his time spent on the deserted island.

☐ **Crouching Tiger, Hidden Dragon (2000):** A young Chinese warrior steals a sword from a famed swordsman and then escapes into a world of romantic adventure with a mysterious man in the frontier of the nation.

☐ **Die Hard (1988):** An NYPD officer tries to save his wife and several others taken hostage by German terrorists during a Christmas party at the Nakatomi Plaza in Los Angeles. **Fun Fact:** Alan Rickman was dropped a second early to get his true reaction to falling from the Nakatomi Plaza in *Die Hard*. **Memorable Quote:** *"Yippie-ki-yay, motherfucker!"*

☐ **Doctor Zhivago (1965):** The life of a Russian physician and poet who, although married to another, falls in love with a political activist's wife and experiences hardship during World War I. **Goof:** In the movie, Varykino is in Siberia, east of Moscow. In real life, the city is west of Moscow.

☐ **Enter the Dragon (1973):** A secret agent comes to an opium lord's island fortress with other fighters for a martial-arts tournament.

☐ **The Fast and Furious (2001):** Los Angeles police officer Brian O'Conner must decide where his loyalty really lies when he becomes enamored with the street racing world he has been sent undercover to destroy. **My Two Cents:** Umm…Paul Walker? Need I say more? May he rest in peace, because he will always be my number one.

☐ **Inception (2010):** A thief who steals corporate secrets through the use of dream-sharing technology is given the inverse task of planting an idea into the mind of a C.E.O. **Fun Fact:** In an interview with 'Entertainment Weekly', Christopher Nolan explained that he based roles of the Inception team similar to roles that are used in filmmaking - Cobb is the Director, Arthur is the Producer, Ariadne is the Production Designer, Eames is the Actor, Saito is the Studio, and Fischer is the Audience. "In trying to write a team-based creative process, I wrote the one I know," said Nolan. **My Two Cents:** I love this movie for the mere fact it's about dreams, and I love analyzing dreams, learning about dreams, and even dream journaling. I find dreams absolutely fascinating.

☐ **Jumanji (1995):** When two kids find and play a magical board game, they release a man trapped in it for decades - and a host of dangers that can only be stopped by finishing the game.

☐ **Life of Pi (2012):** A young man who survives a disaster at sea is hurtled into an epic journey of adventure and discovery. While cast away, he forms an unexpected connection with another survivor: a fearsome Bengal tiger. **Fun Fact:** Ang Lee hired Steven Callahan as a "nautical consultant." In 1982, Callahan survived 76 days adrift on a rubber lifeboat in the Atlantic after his sailboat sank.

☐ **The Lion in Winter (1968):** 1183 A.D.: King Henry II's three sons all want to inherit the throne, but he won't commit to a choice. They and his wife variously plot to force him.

☐ **Master and Commander (2003):** During the Napoleonic Wars, a brash British captain pushes his ship and crew to their limits in pursuit of a formidable French war vessel around South America. **Goof:** The geography of the Galapagos is misrepresented several times, e.g., having the dialog imply that they are next to Isabela Island when they are sailing near Pinnacle Rock, which is on Bartolome.

☐ **Moonrise Kingdom (2012):** A pair of young lovers flee their New England town, which causes a local search party to fan out to find them.

☐ **North by Northwest (1959):** A New York City advertising executive goes on the run after being mistaken for a government agent by a group of foreign spies. **Goof:** The movie that arguably spawned the modern action genre also touts one of cinema's most well-known goofs. It goes down during a climactic scene inside the Mount Rushmore cafeteria, where Eve Kendall pulls out a gun and prepares to shoot Roger Thornhill. Before the gunshot rings out, a young boy in the background is already covering his ears.

☐ **A Passage to India (1984):** Cultural mistrust and false accusations doom a friendship in British colonial India between an Indian doctor, an Englishwoman engaged to marry a city magistrate, and an English educator.

☐ **Pirates of the Caribbean: The Curse of the Black Pearl (2003):** Blacksmith Will Turner teams up with eccentric pirate "Captain" Jack Sparrow to save his love, the governor's daughter, from Jack's former pirate allies, who are now undead. **Fun Fact:** Clothing and smears of charcoal were used to conceal Johnny Depp's numerous tattoos. The "Jack Sparrow" tattoo on his arm in the movie is a fake, but he got a real replica after finishing the film, in honor of his son Jack.

☐ **Indiana Jones Franchise (1981):** In 1936, archaeologist and adventurer Indiana Jones is hired by the U.S. government to find the Ark of the Covenant before Adolf Hitler's Nazis can obtain its awesome powers. **Fun Fact:** Only 12 years separates father/son duo Sean Connery and Harrison Ford in the Indiana Jones franchise.

☐ **Spartacus (1960):** The slave Spartacus leads a violent revolt against the decadent Roman Republic.

☐ **Speed (1994):** A young police officer must prevent a bomb exploding aboard a city bus by keeping its speed above 50 mph. **Goof:** No airport has a dedicated "emergency runway." Also, runways are designated by compass headings, such as 19 right or 31 left, and would not be known as the "Brave Tango" runway. **My**

Two Cents: This movie has the most goofs out of any movie I have watched so far. If you are interested scroll IMDB.com.

☐ **Top Gun (1986):** As students at the United States Navy's elite fighter weapons school compete to be best in the class, one daring young pilot learns a few things from a civilian instructor that are not taught in the classroom. **Memorable Quote:** *"I feel the need – the need for speed!"*

☐ **The Towering Inferno (1974):** At the opening party of a colossal, but poorly constructed, office building, a massive fire breaks out that threatens to destroy the tower and everyone in it.

☐ **The Treasure of the Sierra Madre (1948):** Two Americans searching for work in Mexico convince an old prospector to help them mine for gold in the Sierra Madre Mountains. **Goof:** True to its name, this John Huston adventure takes place in the Sierra Madre mountains of Mexico. But if that's the case, then why is there an Australian kookaburra making noises in the background? **Memorable Quote:** *"Badges? We ain't got no badges! We don't need no badges! I don't have to show you any stinking badges!"*

☐ **Troy (2004):** An adaptation of Homer's great epic, the film follows the assault on Troy by the united Greek forces and chronicles the fates of the men involved.

☐ **True Lies (1994):** A fearless, globe-trotting, terrorist-battling secret agent has his life turned upside down when he discovers his wife might be having an affair with a used-car salesman while terrorists smuggle nuclear war heads into the United States. **My Two Cents:** Jamie Lee Curtis dancing might be the most memorable scene of all-time in my eyes.

☐ **War and Peace (1956):** Napoleon's tumultuous relations with Russia, including his disastrous 1812 invasion, serve as the backdrop for the tangled personal lives of two aristocratic families.

Animation

Animation is a method in which figures are manipulated to appear as moving images. In traditional animation, images are drawn or painted by hand on transparent celluloid sheets to be photographed and exhibited on film. Today, most animations are made with computer-generated imagery (CGI). Computer animation can be very detailed 3D animation, while 2D computer animation (which may have the look of traditional animation) can be used for stylistic reasons, low bandwidth, or faster real-time renderings. Other common animation methods apply a stop motion technique to two and three-dimensional objects like paper cutouts, puppets, or clay figures.

Commonly, the effect of animation is achieved by a rapid succession of sequential images that minimally differ from each other. The illusion—as in motion pictures in general—is thought to rely on the phi phenomenon and beta movement, but the exact causes are still uncertain. Analog mechanical animation media that rely on the rapid display of sequential images include the phénakisticope, zoetrope, flip book, praxinoscope, and film. Television and video are popular electronic animation media that originally were analog and now operate digitally. For display on the computer, techniques like animated GIF and Flash animation were developed.

☐ **All Dogs Go to Heaven (1989):** A canine angel, Charlie, sneaks back to earth from heaven but ends up befriending an orphan girl who can speak to animals. In the process, Charlie learns that friendship is the most heavenly gift of all. **Goof:** Charlie brings pizza to Flo and her pups. Pizza would have been unknown in New Orleans in 1939. It did not become popular all over the United States until after World War II.

☐ **An American Tail (1986):** While emigrating to the United States, a young Russian mouse gets separated from his family and must relocate them while trying to survive in a new country.

☐ **Anastasia (1997):** The last surviving child of the Russian Royal Family joins two con men to reunite with her grandmother, the Dowager Empress, while the undead Rasputin seeks her death. **My Favorite Song:** "Once Upon a December."

☐ **Balto (1995):** An outcast Husky risks his life with other sled dogs to prevent a deadly epidemic from ravaging Nome, Alaska.

☐ **The Brave Little Toaster (1987):** A group of dated appliances embark on a journey to the city to find their master after being abandoned in a cabin in the woods. **Fun Fact:** In a 2010 interview at Cal State, Northridge, Deanna Oliver revealed that at her son's deployment ceremony to Afghanistan, some of the soldiers who were fans of the film had brought their toasters with them for her to autograph.

☐ **Cloudy with a Chance of Meatballs (2009):** A local scientist is often regarded as a failure until he invents a machine that can make food fall from the sky. But little does he know, that things are about to take a turn for the worst.

☐ **Despicable Me (2010):** When a criminal mastermind uses a trio of orphan girls as pawns for a grand scheme, he finds their love is profoundly changing him for the better. **Fun Fact:** Directors Pierre Coffin and Chris Renaud wrote a language for the gibberish the minions speak throughout this movie. They called it "minion-ese". Each word the minions speak in this movie translates into an actual word.

☐ **FernGully: The Last Rainforest (1992):** The magical inhabitants of a rainforest fight to save their home, which is threatened by logging and a polluting force of destruction called Hexxus. **My Two Cents:** This is the first animation movie I remember watching as a little kid.

☐ **Grave of the Fireflies (1988):** A young boy and his little sister struggle to survive in Japan during World War II.

☐ **Happy Feet (2006):** Into the world of the Emperor Penguins, who find their soul mates through song, a penguin is born who cannot sing. But he can tap dance something fierce! **Memorable Quote:** *"Just a moment. I hear people wanting something... ME!"*

☐ **How to Train Your Dragon (2010):** A hapless young Viking who aspires to hunt dragons becomes the unlikely friend of a young dragon himself, and learns there may be more to the creatures than he assumed.

☐ **Ice Age (2002):** The story revolves around sub-zero heroes: a woolly mammoth, a saber-toothed tiger, a sloth and a prehistoric combination of a squirrel and rat, known as Scrat. **Goof:** While escaping from the lava, Manny at one point makes a jump to get over a chasm. Elephants, and by extension mammoths, are of the few mammals that can't jump.

☐ **Inside Out (2015):** After young Riley is uprooted from her Midwest life and moved to San Francisco, her emotions - Joy, Fear, Anger, Disgust and Sadness - conflict on how best to navigate a new city, house, and school.

☐ **The Iron Giant (1999):** A young boy befriends a giant robot from outer space that a paranoid government agent wants to destroy. **Goof:** At the beginning of the film, Sputnik is shown orbiting from East to West. All non-polar orbits of satellites run West to East, in order to take advantage of the Earth's rotation.

☐ **Klaus (2019):** A simple act of kindness always sparks another, even in a frozen, faraway place. When Smeerensburg's new postman, Jesper, befriends toymaker Klaus, their gifts melt an age-old feud and deliver a sleigh full of holiday traditions.

☐ **Kung Fu Panda (2008):** The Dragon Warrior has to clash against the savage Tai Lung as China's fate hangs in the balance. However, the Dragon Warrior mantle is supposedly mistaken to be bestowed upon an obese panda who is a novice in martial arts. **Fun Fact:** The animators took a six-hour kung fu class to get an idea of the movie's action.

☐ **The Land Before Time (1988):** An orphaned brontosaurus teams up with other young dinosaurs in order to reunite with their families in a valley. **Sad Fact:** Judith Barsi, who did the voice for Ducky, was murdered by her father four months before the film's release. Judith was only ten years old. Her headstone includes her famous line in this film, "Yep! Yep! Yep!"

☐ **Mary and Max (2009):** A tale of friendship between two unlikely pen pals: Mary, a lonely, eight-year-old girl living in the suburbs of Melbourne, and Max, a forty-four-year-old, severely obese man living in New York.

☐ **The Pagemaster (1994):** A cowardly boy, who buries himself in accident statistics, enters a library to escape a storm, only to be transformed into an animated illustration by the Pagemaster. He has to work through obstacles from classic books to return to real-life. **Fun Fact:** This movie took almost three and a half years to complete.

☐ **The Polar Express (2004):** On Christmas Eve, a young boy embarks on a magical adventure to the North Pole on the Polar Express, while learning about friendship, bravery, and the spirit of Christmas.

☐ **The Prince of Egypt (1998):** Egyptian Prince Moses learns of his identity as a Hebrew and his destiny to become the chosen deliverer of his people. **Fun Fact:** The voice of God, to avoid controversy, was played by all of the major actors. The actors were told to whisper the lines, so none would dominate the performance, but by the time they got around to having Val Kilmer read his lines, they realized they needed someone to be louder. You still can hear the rest of the cast whispering beneath Kilmer's voice in God's lines.

☐ **Rio (2011):** When Blu, a domesticated macaw from small-town Minnesota, meets the fiercely independent Jewel, he takes off on an adventure to Rio de Janeiro with the bird of his dreams.

☐ **The Secret of NIMH (1982):** To save her ill son, a field mouse must seek the aid of a colony of rats, with whom she has a deeper link than she ever suspected. **Fun Fact:** At the time of release, it was the largest non-Disney animated movie.

☐ **Secret Life of Pets (2016):** The quiet life of a terrier named Max is upended when his owner takes in Duke, a stray whom Max instantly dislikes.

☐ **Shrek (2001):** A mean lord exiles fairytale creatures to the swamp of a grumpy ogre, who must go on a quest and rescue a princess for the lord in order to get his land back. **Memorable Quote:** *"That must be Lord Farquaad's castle... Do you think he's maybe compensating for something?"*

☐ **Shark Tale (2004):** When a son of a gangster shark boss is accidentally killed while on the hunt, his would-be prey and his vegetarian brother decide to use the incident to their own advantage.

☐ **Spirited Away (2001):** During her family's move to the suburbs, a sullen 10-year-old girl wanders into a world ruled by gods, witches, and spirits, and where humans are changed into beasts. **Goof:** Praised for its detailed animation, the film still slips a couple of times when it comes to continuity. For example, the smudge of dirt on Chihiro's face moves around and changes shape and size for the first third of the movie before sticking in one place.

☐ **Song of the Sea (2014):** Ben, a young Irish boy, and his little sister Saoirse, a girl who can turn into a seal, go on an adventure to free the fairies and save the spirit world.

☐ **Soul (2020):** After landing the gig of a lifetime, a New York jazz pianist suddenly finds himself trapped in a strange land between Earth and the afterlife. **Fun Fact:** Animators used footage of several music performers, including jazz composer Jon Batiste, performing as reference for the film's musical sequences. By capturing MIDI data from the sessions, animators were able to retrace the exact key being played on the piano with each note and create the performances authentically.

- ☐ **Thumbelina (1994):** This retelling of the Hans Christian Andersen classic fairy tale has the digit-sized heroine evading the clutches of various toads, moles, and beetles before she can proceed with her courtship with her dream lover, Prince Cornelius.

Biographical/Historical

A historical film is a fiction film showing past events or set within a historical period. This extensive genre shares territory with the biopic, costume drama, heritage film, and epic film.

- ☐ **All the President's Men (1976):** "The Washington Post" reporters Bob Woodward and Carl Bernstein uncover the details of the Watergate scandal that leads to President Richard Nixon's resignation **Goof:** The name of the lawyer encountered by Woodward at the arraignment of the Watergate burglars gives his name as "Markham." In reality, the lawyer identified himself to Woodward as Douglas Caddy.

- ☐ **American Sniper (2014):** Navy S.E.A.L. sniper Chris Kyle's pinpoint accuracy saves countless lives on the battlefield and turns him into a legend. Back home with his family after four tours of duty, however, Chris finds that it is the war he can't leave behind.

- ☐ **Amistad (1997):** In 1839, the revolt of Mende captives aboard a Spanish owned ship causes a major controversy in the United States when the ship is captured off the coast of Long Island. The courts must decide whether the Mende are slaves or legally free. **Fun Fact:** Sir Anthony Hopkins astounded the crew by delivering the entire seven-page courtroom speech in a single take. Steven Spielberg was so in awe, he couldn't bring himself to call him Tony, and insisted on addressing him as Sir Anthony throughout the shoot.

- ☐ **An Angel at My Table (1990):** Janet Frame was a brilliant child who, as a teen, was misdiagnosed with schizophrenia. Explore

Janet's discovery of the world and her life in Europe as her books are published to acclaim.

☐ **Apollo 13 (1995):** NASA must devise a strategy to return Apollo 13 to Earth safely after the spacecraft undergoes massive internal damage putting the lives of the three astronauts on board in jeopardy. **Misquote:** "Houston, we have a problem." **Actual Quote:** "Ah, Houston, *we've had* a problem."

☐ **The Aviator (2005):** A biopic depicting the early years of legendary Director and aviator Howard Hughes' career from the late 1920s to the mid-1940s.

☐ **The Big Short (2015):** In 2006-2007 a group of investors bet against the US mortgage market. In their research they discover how flawed and corrupt the market is. **Goof:** The quote in the opening credits attributed to Mark Twain was actually from Josh Billings, a 19th-century American humorist.

☐ **Birdman of Alcatraz (1962):** A surly convicted murderer held in permanent isolation redeems himself when he becomes a renowned bird expert.

☐ **BlacKkKlansman (2018):** Ron Stallworth, an African American police officer from Colorado Springs, CO, successfully manages to infiltrate the local Ku Klux Klan branch with the help of a Jewish surrogate who eventually becomes its leader. Based on actual events. **Fun Fact:** The real Ron Stallworth had originally wanted Denzel Washington to play him, but was ecstatic to find out his son got the role.

☐ **The Boy Who Harnessed the Wind (2019):** Against all the odds, a thirteen-year-old boy in Malawi invents an unconventional way to save his family and village from famine.

☐ **Capote (2005):** In 1959, Truman Capote learns of the murder of a Kansas family and decides to write a book about the case. While researching for his novel In Cold Blood, Capote forms a relationship with one of the killers, Perry Smith, who is on death row. **Goof:** Although depicted in several scenes typing furiously on a typewriter, Truman Capote was famous for writing everything in longhand. He never typed any of his novels or short stories.

☐ **Catch Me If You Can (2002):** Barely 21 yet, Frank is a skilled forger who has passed as a doctor, lawyer and pilot. FBI agent Carl becomes obsessed with tracking down the con man, who only revels in the pursuit. **Fun Fact:** The real Frank Abagnale Jr. appears in *Catch Me If You Can* as the French policeman who arrests Leo.

☐ **Coal Miner's Daughter (1980):** The life of legendary Loretta Lynn, the dirt-poor Appalachian Mountains girl who rose from humble beginnings to become the "Queen of Country Music."

☐ **Dallas Buyer's Club (2013):** In 1985 Dallas, electrician and hustler Ron Woodroof works around the system to help AIDS patients get the medication they need after he is diagnosed with the disease. **Fun Fact:** The film's budget was so low that the makeup budget was $250. The film's artists were able to work with that, and the film's Makeup and Hairstyling won an Oscar.

☐ **Donnie Brasco (1997):** An FBI undercover agent infiltrates the mob and finds himself identifying more with the mafia life, at the expense of his regular one.

☐ **The Elephant Man (1980):** A Victorian surgeon rescues a heavily disfigured man who is mistreated while scraping a living as a side-show freak. Behind his monstrous façade, there is revealed a person of kindness, intelligence and sophistication. **Fun Fact:** David Lynch was working as a roofer at the time he was offered the chance to direct.

☐ **Ford v. Ferrari (2019):** American car designer Carroll Shelby and driver Ken Miles battle corporate interference and the laws of physics to build a revolutionary race car for Ford in order to defeat Ferrari at the 24 Hours of Le Mans in 1966.

☐ **The Founder (2016):** The story of Ray Kroc, a salesman who turned two brothers' innovative fast-food eatery, McDonald's, into the biggest restaurant business in the world, with a combination of ambition, persistence, and ruthlessness. **Fun Fact:** The company Kroc worked for prior to founding McDonald's, Prince Castle, still exists, and supplies McDonald's with much of its equipment.

☐ **Frida (2002):** A biography of artist Frida Kahlo, who channeled the pain of a crippling injury and her tempestuous marriage into her work.

☐ **Frost/Nixon (2008):** A dramatic retelling of the post-Watergate television interviews between British talk-show host David Frost and former president Richard Nixon. **Fun Fact:** Kevin Bacon said the day Ron Howard called him about being cast in *Frost/Nixon*, Bacon had tickets to a production of the play for that very same night.

☐ **Glory (1989):** Robert Gould Shaw leads the U.S. Civil War's first all-black volunteer company, fighting prejudices from both his own Union Army, and the Confederates.

☐ **The Great Debaters (2007):** A drama based on the true story of Melvin B. Tolson, a professor at Wiley College Texas. In 1935, he inspired students to form the school's first debate team, which went on to challenge Harvard in the national championship. **Fun Fact:** On December 19, 2007, Denzel Washington announced a $1 million dollar gift to Wiley College, so they could re-establish their debate team.

☐ **Hacksaw Ridge (2016):** World War II American Army Medic Desmond T. Doss, who served during the Battle of Okinawa, refuses to kill people and becomes the first man in American history to receive the Medal of Honor without firing a shot.

☐ **Hidden Figures (2016):** The story of a team of female African-American mathematicians who served a vital role in NASA during the early years of the U.S. space program. **Goof:** The manual for the IBM 7090 computer has an incorrect logo for IBM. The dashed IBM logo was not introduced until 1972.

☐ **Hotel Rwanda (2004):** Paul Rusesabagina, a hotel manager, houses over a thousand Tutsi refugees during their struggle against the Hutu militia in Rwanda, Africa.

☐ **The Imitation Game (2014):** During World War II, the English mathematical genius Alan Turing tries to crack the German Enigma code with help from fellow mathematicians. **Fun Fact:** Benedict Cumberbatch confessed that in one of the final scenes of the film, he couldn't stop crying and had a breakdown. It was, as he said, "Being an actor or a person that had grown incredibly fond of the character and thinking what he had suffered and how that had affected him."

☐ **In Cold Blood (1967):** After a botched robbery results in the brutal murder of a rural family, two drifters elude police, in the end coming to terms with their own mortality and the repercussions of their vile atrocity.

☐ **Inherit the Wind (1960):** Based on a real-life case in 1925, two great lawyers argue the case for and against a science teacher accused of the crime of teaching evolution. **Memorable Quote:** *"I don't swear just for the hell of it. Language is a poor enough means of communication. I think we should use all the words we've got. Besides, there are damn few words that anybody understands."*

☐ **In the Name of the Father (1993):** A man's coerced confession to an I.R.A. bombing he did not commit results in the imprisonment of his father as well. An English lawyer fights to free them.

☐ **Into the Wild (2007):** After graduating from Emory University, top student and athlete Christopher McCandless abandons his possessions, gives his entire $24,000 savings account to charity and hitchhikes to Alaska to live in the wilderness. Along the way, Christopher encounters a series of characters that shape his life. **Fun Fact:** The temperature outdoors was at freezing when Emile Hirsch performed the naked back float down the stream.

☐ **The Irishman (2019):** Hitman Frank Sheeran looks back at the secrets he kept as a loyal member of the Bufalino crime family.

☐ **I, Tonya (2017):** Competitive ice skater Tonya Harding rises amongst the ranks at the U.S. Figure Skating Championships, but her future in the activity is thrown into doubt when her ex-husband intervenes. **Goof:** When Tonya Harding competed, song lyrics were not allowed in competition the way they are today. Although she included "Sleeping Bag" by ZZ Top in the 3d section of her 1991-1992 program, it was the music only.

☐ **JFK (1991):** New Orleans District Attorney Jim Garrison discovers there's more to the Kennedy assassination than the official story.

☐ **The Killing Fields (1984):** A journalist is trapped in Cambodia during tyrant Pol Pot's bloody 'Year Zero' cleansing campaign, which claimed the lives of two million 'undesirable' civilians. **Fun Fact:** In real life, Haing S. Ngor's wife died under the Khmer Rouge regime, hemorrhaging during childbirth (the baby also died). She knew that she couldn't contact her husband as doctors were all being murdered by the regime so by keeping her silence and dying of internal bleeding, she effectively saved his life.

☐ **Lincoln (2012):** As the American Civil War continues to rage, America's president struggles with continuing carnage on the battlefield as he fights with many inside his own cabinet on the decision to emancipate the slaves.

☐ **Love and Mercy (2014):** In the 60s, Beach Boys leader Brian Wilson struggles with emerging psychosis as he attempts to craft his avant-garde pop masterpiece. In the 80s, he is a broken, confused man under the 24-hour watch of shady therapist Dr. Eugene Landy. **Memorable Quote:** *"I want you to leave, but I don't want you to leave me."*

☐ **Malcolm X (1992):** Biographical epic of the controversial and influential Black Nationalist leader, from his early life and career as a small-time gangster, to his ministry as a member of the Nation of Islam.

☐ **The Miracle Worker (1962):** The story of Anne Sullivan's struggle to teach the blind and deaf Helen Keller how to communicate. **Goof:** Anne Bancroft plays Annie Sullivan with a slight Irish accent. The real Sullivan was born in Agawam, Massachusetts and had no such accent.

☐ **My Left Foot (1989):** Christy Brown, born with cerebral palsy, learns to paint and write with his only controllable limb - his left foot. **Fun Fact:** Daniel Day-Lewis broke two ribs during filming from assuming the hunched-over position in his wheelchair for weeks of filming. He also would refuse to come out of character. On visits to the set canteen, other people would have to help him with food.

☐ **The Passion of Joan of Arc (1928):** In 1431, Jeanne d'Arc is placed on trial on charges of heresy. The ecclesiastical jurists attempt to force Jeanne to recant her claims of holy visions.

☐ **The Pianist (2002):** A Polish Jewish musician struggles to survive the destruction of the Warsaw ghetto of World War II. **Fun Fact:** Notice how director of photography Pawel Edelman slowly drains the color out of all the scenes as the film progresses to signify the deterioration of the city and of Szpilman himself.

☐ **The Post (2017):** A cover-up spanning four U.S. Presidents pushes the country's first female newspaper publisher and her editor to join an unprecedented battle between press and government.

☐ **Pride (2014):** U.K. gay activists work to help miners during their lengthy strike of the National Union of Mineworkers in the summer of 1984. **Goof:** On Joe's birthday, in July 1984, a record of 'What Difference Does It Make?' by The Smiths can be heard. Whilst the original song was released in 1983, the version playing in the film was one recorded for the BBC, which was not actually released until November 1984.

☐ **The Pursuit of Happyness (2006):** A struggling salesman takes custody of his son as he's poised to begin a life-changing professional career.

☐ **Quiz Show (1994):** A young lawyer, Richard Goodwin, investigates a potentially fixed game show. Charles Van Doren, a big time show winner, is under Goodwin's investigation. **Memorable Quote:** *"Sixty-four thousand dollars for a question, I hope they are asking you the meaning of life."*

☐ **Selma (2014):** A chronicle of Dr. Martin Luther King, Jr.'s campaign to secure equal voting rights via an epic march from Selma to Montgomery, Alabama, in 1965.

☐ **The Sea Inside (2004):** The factual story of Spaniard Ramon Sampedro, who fought a thirty-year campaign in favor of euthanasia and his own right to die. **Fun Fact:** This is the second Spanish movie about Ramon Sampedro's life. The first one was *Condenado a vivir* (2001).

☐ **Searching for Bobby Fischer (1993):** A prepubescent chess prodigy refuses to harden himself in order to become a champion like the famous but unlikable Bobby Fischer.

☐ **Shine (1996):** Pianist David Helfgott, driven by his father and teachers, has a breakdown. Years later he returns to the piano, to popular if not critical acclaim. **Memorable Quote:** *"You must play as if there's no tomorrow."*

☐ **The Social Network (2010):** As Harvard student Mark Zuckerberg creates the social networking site that would become known as Facebook, he is sued by the twins who claimed he stole their idea, and by the co-founder who was later squeezed out of the business.

☐ **The Theory of Everything (2014):** A look at the relationship between the famous physicist Stephen Hawking and his wife. **Fun Fact:** Eddie Redmayne met with Stephen Hawking only once before filming. "In the three hours I spent with him, he said maybe eight sentences," recalls Redmayne. "I just didn't feel like I could ask him intimate things." Therefore, he found other ways to prepare for the role. He lost about 15 pounds and trained for four months with a dancer to learn how to control his body. He met with 40 ALS patients, kept a chart tracking the order in which Hawking's muscles declined, and stood in front of a mirror for hours on end, contorting his face. Lastly, he remained motionless and hunched over between takes, so much so that an osteopath told him he had altered the alignment of his spine.

☐ **The Wolf of Wall Street (2013):** Based on the true story of Jordan Belfort, from his rise to a wealthy stock-broker living the high life to his fall involving crime, corruption and the federal government. **Fun Fact:** The actors snorted crushed B vitamins for scenes that involved cocaine. Jonah Hill claimed that he eventually became sick with bronchitis after so much inhaling and had to be hospitalized.

☐ **127 Hours (2010):** A mountain climber becomes trapped under a boulder while canyoneering alone near Moab, Utah and resorts to desperate measures in order to survive.

Comedy

Ahhh…comedy, my favorite genre to write and watch. There is nothing like a good laugh to soothe your soul. There are so many, and I know I forgot some as this list got way longer than I wanted it to. I only wanted 1,000 films, but I ended up with over 1,215, and then I added some more as I realized I forgot some of my own personal favorites. If I forgot any comedy classics, please, please, please let me know! Read the introduction on how to contact me.

☐ **Airplane! (1980):** A man afraid to fly must ensure that a plane lands safely after the pilots become sick. **Memorable Quote:** *"Surely you can't be serious." "I am serious…and don't call me Shirley."*

☐ **All of Me (1984):** A dying millionaire has her soul transferred into a younger, willing woman. However, something goes wrong, and she finds herself in her lawyer's body - together with the lawyer.

☐ **Anchorman (2004):** Ron Burgundy is San Diego's top-rated newsman in the male-dominated broadcasting of the 1970s, but that's all about to change for Ron and his cronies when an ambitious woman is hired as a new anchor. **My Favorite Line:** *"You've got a dirty whorish mouth."*

☐ **Animal House (1978):** At a 1962 college, Dean Vernon Wormer is determined to expel the entire Delta Tau Chi Fraternity, but those troublemakers have other plans for him.

☐ **Arsenic and Old Lace (1943):** A writer of books on the futility of marriage risks his reputation when he decides to get married. Things get even more complicated when he learns on his wedding day that his beloved maiden aunts are habitual murderers. **Fun**

Fact: The movie opens with the Brooklyn Dodgers winning a baseball game on Halloween, weeks after the end of baseball season. This is a gag to suggest that the only time the Brooklyn Dodgers could win is on Halloween, similar to saying when pigs fly.

☐ **Austin Powers (1997):** A world-class playboy and part-time secret agent from the 1960s emerges after thirty years in a cryogenic state to battle with his nemesis Dr. Evil.

☐ **Best in Show (2000):** A behind-the-scenes look into the highly competitive and cut-throat world of dog shows through the eyes of a group of ruthless dog owners. **Fun Fact:** Fred Willard (Buck Laughlin) was specifically instructed by Christopher Guest to not do any research on dogs. Jim Piddock (Trevor Beckwith), on the other hand, had to do a lot of dog research so that his character would appear knowledgeable. As a result, Guest says some viewers are surprised to learn Piddock is not a real dog show judge.

☐ **The Big Lebowski (1998):** Jeff "The Dude" Lebowski, mistaken for a millionaire of the same name, seeks restitution for his ruined rug and enlists his bowling buddies to help get it. **Fun Fact:** The check The Dude fills out at Ralph's in *The Big Lebowski* is dated September 11th 1991.

☐ **The Birdcage (1996):** A gay cabaret owner and his drag queen companion agree to put up a false straight front so that their son can introduce them to his fiancée's right-wing moralistic parents.

☐ **Blazing Saddles (1974):** In order to ruin a western town, a corrupt politician appoints a black Sheriff, who promptly becomes his most formidable adversary. **Fun Fact:** Mel Brooks never told Frankie Laine that the theme song "Blazing Saddles" was for a comedy. Laine thought it was a dramatic western. Brooks was worried that Laine wouldn't sing it with conviction if he knew the truth.

☐ **Bluebeard's Eighth Wife (1938):** After learning her multi-millionaire fiancé has already been married seven times, the daughter of a penniless marquis decides to tame him.

- ☐ **Born Yesterday (1950):** A tycoon hires a tutor to teach his lover proper etiquette, with unexpected results. **My Two Cents:** This is one of my favorite Judy Holliday movies, along with *It Should Happen to You.* (That is not on this list, but you should check it out when you decide to go on a classic movie binge.)

- ☐ **Bringing Up Baby (1938):** While trying to secure a $1 million donation for his museum, a befuddled paleontologist is pursued by a flighty and often irritating heiress and her pet leopard, Baby.

- ☐ **Broadcast News (1987):** Take two rival television reporters: one handsome, one talented, both male. Add one Producer, female. Mix well, and watch the sparks fly. **Goof:** After the special report is completed, everyone heads out to have a drink and celebrate. In reality, all of the reporters would have had to continue working long enough to produce a report for the evening news - even on a Sunday.

- ☐ **Caddyshack (1980):** An exclusive golf course has to deal with a brash new member and a destructive dancing gopher. **Memorable Quote:** *"Cinderella story. Outta nowhere. A former greenskeeper, now, about to become the Masters champion. It looks like a miracle...It's in the hole! It's in the hole! It's in the Hole!"*

- ☐ **City Lights (1931):** With the aid of a wealthy erratic tippler, a dewy-eyed tramp who has fallen in love with a sightless flower girl accumulates money to be able to help her medically. **Goof:** Admittedly, films like 1931's *City Lights* were shot in technologically humble times for Hollywood. Though Charlie Chaplin built his legacy in intended comedy, numerous errors slipped through the cracks of his movies in a more indirectly hilarious fashion. Despite a budget of $1.5 million, Chaplin and Co. struggled to fill a gallery of spectators for the famous fight scene. If you watch the back row, you'll notice nobody is moving due to the use of cut-outs, mannequins, and even painted-on people. You can actually spot the same mannequin of a man in a gray suit in several scenes in *City Lights.*

☐ **Coming to America (1988):** An extremely pampered African prince travels to Queens, New York, and goes undercover to find a wife that he can respect for her intelligence and strong will. **Fun Fact:** This was the first time Eddie Murphy played multiple characters in the same film, which became a trademark of his.

☐ **Deadpool (2016):** A wisecracking mercenary gets experimented on and becomes immortal but ugly, and sets out to track down the man who ruined his looks.

☐ **Dirty Rotten Scoundrels (1988):** Two con men try to settle their rivalry by betting on who can swindle a young American heiress out of fifty thousand dollars first. **Memorable Quote:** *"Ruprecht, do you want the genital cuff?"*

☐ **Duck Soup (1933):** Rufus T. Firefly is named president/dictator of bankrupt Freedonia and declares war on neighboring Sylvania over the love of wealthy Mrs. Teasdale.

☐ **Dumb and Dumber (1994):** After a woman leaves a briefcase at the airport terminal, a dumb limo driver and his dumber friend set out on a hilarious cross-country road trip to Aspen to return it. **My Favorite Line:** *"We got no food. We got no jobs. Our pets' heads are falling off."*

☐ **A Fish Called Wanda (1988):** In London, four very different people team up to commit armed robbery, then try to double-cross each other for the loot.

☐ **The Fortune Cookie (1966):** A crooked lawyer persuades his brother-in-law to feign a serious injury. **Fun Fact:** Jack Lemmon and Walter Matthau bonded early in the production process, finding a connection in their mutual love of football. They would remain friends the rest of their lives.

☐ **The 40-Year-Old Virgin (2005):** Goaded by his buddies, a nerdy guy who's never "done the deed" only finds the pressure mounting when he meets a single mother.

☐ **Four Weddings and a Funeral (1994):** Over the course of five social occasions, a committed bachelor must consider the notion that he may have discovered love. **Fun Fact:** Inspiration for this movie came when co-executive producer and writer Richard Curtis was flipping through some old diaries and realized that he had been to seventy-two weddings in ten years.

☐ **The General (1926):** When Union spies steal an engineer's beloved locomotive, he pursues it single-handedly and straight through enemy lines.

☐ **The Gold Rush (1925):** A prospector goes to the Klondike in search of gold and finds it and more. **Memorable Quotes:** *"Blissful ignorance."*

☐ **The Grand Budapest Hotel (2014):** A writer encounters the owner of an aging high-class hotel, who tells him of his early years serving as a lobby boy in the hotel's glorious years under an exceptional concierge.

☐ **The Great Dictator (1940):** Dictator Adenoid Hynkel tries to expand his empire while a poor Jewish barber tries to avoid persecution from Hynkel's regime. **Fun Fact:** Adolf Hitler banned the film in Germany and in all countries occupied by the Nazis. Curiosity got the best of him, and he had a print brought in through Portugal. History records that he screened it twice, in private, but history did not record his reaction to the film. Charles Chaplin said, "I'd give anything to know what he thought of it." For political reasons in Germany, the ban stayed after the end of WWII until 1958.

☐ **Grosse Pointe Blank (1997):** Martin Blank is a professional assassin. He is sent on a mission to a small Detroit suburb, Grosse Pointe, and, by coincidence, his ten-year high school reunion party is taking place there at the same time.

☐ **Groundhog Day (1993):** A weatherman finds himself inexplicably living the same day over and over again. **Memorable Quote:** *"Well, what if there is no tomorrow? There wasn't one today."*

☐ **The Hangover (2009):** Three buddies wake up from a bachelor party in Las Vegas, with no memory of the previous night and the bachelor missing. They make their way around the city in order to find their friend before his wedding. **Fun Fact:** In *The Hangover*, Ed Helms is actually missing a tooth. He never had an adult incisor grow, and his fake incisor was taken out for the parts of filming where Stu's tooth is missing. **My Favorite Line:** *"Hey guys, you ready to let the dogs out?"* This has to be done while also simulating the dance.

☐ **His Girl Friday (1940):** A newspaper editor uses every trick in the book to keep his ace reporter ex-wife from remarrying.

☐ **Horse Feathers (1932):** Quincy Adams Wagstaff, the new president of Huxley University, accidentally hires bumblers Baravelli and Pinky to help his school win the big football game against the rival Darwin University. **Fun Fact:** Before she became famous, Shirley Temple walked by the set with her parents at one point during filming. Harpo Marx reportedly approached her parents with an offer to adopt the child on the spot for $50,000.

☐ **I Heart Huckabees (2004):** A husband-and-wife team play detective, but not in the traditional sense. Instead, the happy duo helps others solve their existential issues, the kind that keep you up at night, wondering what it all means.

☐ **In the Loop (2009):** A political satire about a group of skeptical American and British operatives attempting to prevent a war between two countries. **Goof:** Toby mentions he met Liza while she was a Kennedy scholar at his college in Cambridge. In reality, Kennedy Scholarships are for British students to study at Harvard or MIT.

☐ **Kind Hearts and Coronets (1949):** A distant poor relative of the Duke D'Ascoyne plots to inherit the title by murdering the eight other heirs who stand ahead of him in the line of succession.

☐ **Liar Liar (1997):** A fast-track lawyer can't lie for 24 hours due to his son's birthday wish after he disappoints his son for the last time. **My Favorite Line:** *"I'm kickin' my own ass, d'ya mind?"*

☐ **Life of Brian (1979):** Born on the original Christmas in the stable next door to Jesus Christ, Brian of Nazareth spends his life being mistaken for a messiah.

☐ **Lost in America (1985):** A husband and wife in their 30s decide to quit their jobs, live as free spirits and cruise America in a Winnebago. **Goof:** They never would have been able to pull into New York City and find a Winnebago-sized parking space right in front of the ad agency just like that.

☐ **Meet the Parents (2000):** Male nurse Greg Focker meets his girlfriend's parents before proposing, but her suspicious father is every date's worst nightmare. **Memorable Quote:** *"I have nipples, Greg, could you milk me?"*

☐ **Miss Congeniality (2000):** An F.B.I. Agent must go undercover in the Miss United States beauty pageant to prevent a group from bombing the event.

☐ **Modern Times (1936):** The Tramp struggles to live in modern industrial society with the help of a young homeless woman. **Goof:** When Charlie Chaplin famously emerges from the giant machine, for instance, the footage is played backward. If not for the men behind Chaplin hammering in reverse, the audience would be none the wiser.

☐ **Monty Python and the Holy Grail (1975):** King Arthur and his Knights of the Round Table embark on a surreal, low-budget search for the Holy Grail, encountering many, very silly obstacles.

☐ **Move Over, Darling (1963):** After having been lost at sea for several years, a missing wife thought long dead returns just after her husband has remarried. **Fun Fact:** The movie Ellen (Doris Day) describes to Bianca (Polly Bergen) while giving her a massage is *My Favorite Wife* (1940), of which this is a remake.

☐ **My Cousin Vinny (1992):** Two New Yorkers accused of murder in rural Alabama while on their way back to college call in the help of one of their cousins, a loudmouth lawyer with no trial experience. **My Favorite Line:** *"Uh... everything that guy just said is bullshit... Thank you."*

☐ **The Naked Gun (1988):** Incompetent police Detective Frank Drebin must foil an attempt to assassinate Queen Elizabeth II.

☐ **National Lampoon's Vacation (1983):** The Griswold family's cross-country drive to the Walley World theme park proves to be much more arduous than they ever anticipated. **Fun Fact:** Originally, the producers wanted Christie Brinkley to appear naked in the film, but she refused. A compromise was reached, where she stripped down to her bra and panties before jumping in the pool with Clark.

☐ **National Lampoon's Van Wilder (2002):** The most popular kid on campus meets a beautiful journalist who makes him realize that maybe he's afraid to graduate.

☐ **Nothing Sacred (1937):** An eccentric woman learns she is not dying of radium poisoning as earlier assumed, but when she meets a reporter looking for a story, she feigns sickness again for her own profit. **Fun Fact:** Originally, the producers wanted Christie Brinkley to appear naked in the film, but she refused. A compromise was reached, where she stripped down to her bra and panties before jumping in the pool with Clark.

☐ **The Odd Couple (1968):** Two friends try sharing an apartment, but their ideas of housekeeping and lifestyles are as different as night and day.

☐ **Old School (2003):** Three friends attempt to recapture their glory days by opening up a fraternity near their alma mater. **Memorable Quotes:** *"We're going streaking!"* **My Favorite Line:** *"Earmuffs."*

☐ **The Pink Panther (1963):** The bumbling Inspector Clouseau travels to Rome to catch a notorious jewel thief known as "The Phantom" before he conducts his most daring heist yet: a princess' priceless diamond with one slight imperfection, known as "The Pink Panther."

☐ **Planes, Trains, and Automobiles (1987):** A man must struggle to travel home for Thanksgiving with a lovable oaf of a shower curtain ring salesman as his only companion. **Fun Fact:** John Hughes, in an interview on the "Those Aren't Pillows" DVD, said he was inspired to write the film's story after an actual flight he was on from New York to Chicago. The flight was diverted to Wichita, Kansas, taking him five days to get home.

☐ **Punch-Drunk Love (2002):** A frustrated Barry Egan calls a phone-sex line to curb his loneliness. Little does he know that he will land in huge trouble and will also jeopardize his relationship with Lena.

☐ **Raising Arizona (1987):** When a childless couple of an ex-con and an ex-cop decide to help themselves to one of another family's quintuplets, their lives become more complicated than they anticipated. **Fun Fact:** According to Ethan Coen, Nicolas Cage was crazy about his Woody Woodpecker haircut and that it reacted to H.I.'s stress level. The bigger the danger he's in, the bigger the wave in his hair gets.

☐ **Road to Morocco (1942):** Two carefree castaways on a desert shore find an Arabian Nights city, where they compete for the luscious Princess Shalmar.

☐ **Safety Last! (1923):** A boy leaves his small country town and heads to the big city to get a job. As soon as he makes it big his sweetheart will join him and marry him. His enthusiasm to get ahead leads to some interesting adventures. **Fun Fact:** Harold

Lloyd first tested the safety precautions for the clock stunt by dropping a dummy onto the mattress below. The dummy bounced off and plummeted to the street below.

☐ **Shaun of the Dead (2004):** A man's uneventful life is disrupted by the zombie apocalypse.

☐ **Sherlock Jr. (1924):** A film projectionist longs to be a detective, and puts his meagre skills to work when he is framed by a rival for stealing his girlfriend's father's pocket watch. **Fun Fact:** Buster Keaton practiced for four months, working with a pool expert, to learn all the trick shots that Sherlock Jr. performs during the pool game. Nevertheless, it took him five days to film all the trick shots, and get them right. When he was finished, all the best trick shots he had filmed were cut together to make it look like Sherlock Jr. was playing one continuous game of pool.

☐ **Show People (1928):** A young lady from Georgia goes to Hollywood in the hopes of becoming an actress.

☐ **Snatch (2000):** Unscrupulous boxing promoters, violent bookmakers, a Russian gangster, incompetent amateur robbers and supposedly Jewish jewelers fight to track down a priceless stolen diamond. **Goof:** In the scene where Avi shoots Bullet-Tooth Tony he is firing at least 10 rounds, but the magazine holds eight rounds. **My Two Cents:** This is my dad's biggest pet peeve in movies, when they should have reloaded the gun. He will literally watch intently and count…

☐ **Some Like it Hot (1959):** When two male musicians witness a mob hit, they flee the state in an all-female band disguised as women, but further complications set in. **Goof:** This 1959 comedy classic set in 1929 delivers an array of choice musical numbers, including Marilyn Monroe's rendition of "I'm Thru with Love." That particular song didn't come out until the 1930s.

☐ **Step Brothers (2008):** Two aimless middle-aged losers still living at home are forced against their will to become roommates when their parents marry. **Fun Fact:** Joaquin Phoenix claims to have seen this film more times than he has seen any other movie.

☐ **Sullivan's Travels (1941):** A Hollywood director, John L Sullivan, sets out to experience life as a poor, homeless person in order to gain relevant life experience for his next movie.

☐ **There's Something about Mary (1998):** A man gets a chance to meet up with his dream girl from high school, even though his date with her back then was a complete disaster. **Memorable Quote:** *"Boy, don't make me open up a can of whoop-ass!"*

☐ **This is Spinal Tap (1984):** Spinal Tap, one of England's loudest bands, is chronicled by film director Marty DiBergi on what proves to be a fateful tour. **Memorable Quote:** *"These go to eleven."*

☐ **This is the End (2013):** Six Los Angeles celebrities are stuck in James Franco's house after a series of devastating events just destroyed the city. Inside, the group not only have to face the apocalypse, but themselves.

☐ **To Be or Not to Be (1942):** During the Nazi occupation of Poland, an acting troupe becomes embroiled in a Polish soldier's efforts to track down a German spy. **Fun Fact:** Because Carole Lombard died in a plane crash while the movie was in post-production, the filmmakers decided to cut out a line that had her character ask, "What can happen in a plane?".

☐ **Tommy Boy (1995):** After his auto-parts tycoon father dies, the overweight, underachieving son teams up with a snide accountant to try and save the family business. **My Favorite Line:** *"Fat guy in a little coat."*

☐ **Tootsie (1982):** Michael Dorsey, an unsuccessful actor, disguises himself as a woman in order to get a role on a trashy hospital soap.

☐ **Trading Places (1983):** A snobbish investor and a wily street con artist find their positions reversed as part of a bet by two callous millionaires. **Goof:** FCOJ is subject to daily trading price movement limits. The 'swings' shown would trigger 'limit up' and 'limit down', and trading would be suspended for the day by NYMEX.

☐ **Waiting for Guffman (1996):** An aspiring director and the marginally talented amateur cast of a hokey small-town Missouri musical production go overboard when they learn that someone from Broadway will be in attendance.

☐ **Waking Ned Devine (1998):** When a lottery winner dies of shock, his fellow townsfolk attempt to claim the money. **Fun Fact:** The original title of the script was Waking Ned Devine. However, distributors insisted on changing it to Waking Ned as they felt the shorter title was more user friendly. American distributors were the only ones to keep the 'Devine'.

☐ **Way Out West (1937):** Stanley and Ollie are enlisted to deliver the deed to a goldmine in a small village, only for it to be stolen.

☐ **Wedding Crashers (2005):** John Beckwith and Jeremy Grey, a pair of committed womanizers who sneak into weddings to take advantage of the romantic tinge in the air, find themselves at odds with one another when John meets and falls for Claire Cleary. **My Favorite Line:** *"We got a stage five clinger!"*

☐ **What About Bob? (1991):** A successful psychotherapist loses his mind after one of his most dependent patients, an obsessive-compulsive neurotic, tracks him down during his family vacation. **My Favorite Line:** *"Baby steps."*

☐ **What's Up, Doc? (1972):** The accidental mix-up of four identical plaid overnight bags leads to a series of increasingly wild and wacky situations.

☐ **Young Frankenstein (1974):** An American grandson of the infamous scientist, struggling to prove that his grandfather was not as insane as people believe, is invited to Transylvania, where he discovers the process that reanimates a dead body. **Goof:** Throughout the film, Frederick is referred to as the grandson or great grandson of Victor Frankenstein. However, Victor was a character from 1818 when the novel was first published, which would make Frederick in the 1930's Victor's great-great-great-great grandson, minimum. **Side Note:** I think that would have made the film funnier to refer to him as such.

☐ **Zoolander (2001):** At the end of his career, a clueless fashion model is brainwashed to kill the Prime Minister of Malaysia.

Crime/Mystery/Suspense/Thriller

As the comedy genre is my favorite to write, there is nothing like a gripping thriller to watch. I wish I could write one. All the twists, turns and plots you don't see coming that just keep you guessing until the bitter end. There is nothing like this thrill to keep you on the edge of your seat.

- ☐ **The Asphalt Jungle (1950):** A major heist goes off as planned, but then double crosses, bad luck and solid police work cause everything to unravel. **Fun Fact:** The poster showing Marilyn Monroe in a purple dress was created much later, after she became a household name. Monroe was basically unknown when the film was made in 1950 and only has a very small role. She certainly wouldn't have been given top billing at the time. In fact, she wasn't named on the original posters at all.
- ☐ **Anatomy of a Murder (1959):** In a murder trial, the defendant says he suffered temporary insanity after the victim raped his wife. What is the truth, and will he win his case?
- ☐ **Basic Instinct (1992):** A police detective investigates a brutal murder that might involve a seductive novelist. **Memorable Quote:** *"You know I don't like to wear any underwear, don't you, Nick?"*
- ☐ **Before I Go to Sleep (2014):** A woman wakes up every day, remembering nothing as a result of a traumatic accident in her past. One day, new terrifying truths emerge that force her to question everyone around her.

☐ **The Big Heat (1953):** Tough cop Dave Bannion takes on a politically powerful crime syndicate. **Memorable Quote:** *"Oh, well, you're about as romantic as a pair of handcuffs."*

☐ **The Big Sleep (1946):** Private detective Philip Marlowe is hired by a wealthy family. Before the complex case is over, he's seen murder, blackmail, and what might be love.

☐ **Bonnie and Clyde (1967):** Bored waitress Bonnie Parker falls in love with an ex-con named Clyde Barrow and together they start a violent crime spree through the country, stealing cars and robbing banks. **Memorable Quote:** *"We rob banks."*

☐ **Bullitt (1968):** An all-guts, no-glory San Francisco cop becomes determined to find the underworld kingpin that killed the witness in his protection.

☐ **The Butterfly Effect (2004):** Evan Treborn suffers blackouts during significant events of his life. As he grows up, he finds a way to remember these lost memories and a supernatural way to alter his life by reading his journal. **Fun Fact:** All of the prison scenes were filmed in a real prison (Washington State) with real prisoners. **My Two Cents:** This is just a movie I love watching, not necessarily on any movie lists, but a damn good film in my book.

☐ **Charade (1963):** Romance and suspense ensue in Paris as a woman is pursued by several men who want a fortune her murdered husband had stolen. Whom can she trust?

☐ **The Conversation (1974):** A paranoid, secretive surveillance expert has a crisis of conscience when he suspects that the couple he is spying on will be murdered. **Fun Fact:** Gene Hackman learned to play the saxophone especially for the film.

☐ **Dark Waters (2019):** A corporate defense attorney takes on an environmental lawsuit against a chemical company that exposes a lengthy history of pollution.

☐ **Dial M for Murder (1954):** A former tennis player tries to arrange his wife's murder after learning of her affair.

☐ **Dirty Harry (1971):** When a madman calling himself "the Scorpio Killer" menaces the city, tough-as-nails San Francisco Police Inspector "Dirty" Harry Callahan is assigned to track down and ferret out the crazed psychopath. **Misquote:** "Do ya feel lucky, punk?" **Actual Quote:** "*You've got to ask yourself one question: 'Do I feel lucky?'* Well, do ya punk?"

☐ **Double Indemnity (1944):** An insurance rep gets talked into a murder/insurance fraud scheme by a sexy housewife. **Goof:** In this classic film noir, insurance salesman Walter Neff (Fred MacMurray) gets lured into a duplicitous scheme by Phyllis Dietrichson (Barbara Stanwyck). Neff is supposed to be a bachelor, but MacMurray's real-life wedding ring can be spotted throughout the film.

☐ **Gaslight (1944):** Years after her aunt was murdered in her home, a young woman moves back into the house with her new husband. However, he has a secret that he will do anything to protect, even if it means driving his wife insane.

☐ **Goldfinger (1964):** While investigating a gold magnate's smuggling, James Bond uncovers a plot to contaminate the Fort Knox gold reserve. **Memorable Quotes:** *"A martini. Shaken, not stirred."*

☐ **Gone Girl (2014):** With his wife's disappearance having become the focus of an intense media circus, a man sees the spotlight turned on him when it's suspected that he may not be innocent. **Fun Fact:** Production of the film had to be shut down for four days, due to Ben Affleck's refusal to follow David Fincher's vision, and wear a New York Yankees cap for a scene where Affleck's character, Nick, is at an airport. The Bostonian actor said to Fincher, "David, I love you, I would do anything for you. But I will not wear a Yankees hat." Eventually, the two settled for Ben's character to wear a Mets cap. Fincher jokingly describes Affleck's actions of this as "entirely unprofessional" in the DVD's audio commentary.

☐ **Goodfellas (1990):** The story of Henry Hill and his life in the mob, covering his relationship with his wife Karen Hill and his mob partners Jimmy Conway and Tommy DeVito. **Memorable Quote:** *"I mean, funny like I'm a clown? I amuse you?"*

☐ **Heat (1995):** A group of professional bank robbers start to feel the heat from police when they unknowingly leave a clue at their latest heist.

☐ **Inside Man (2006):** A police detective, a bank robber, and a high-power broker enter high-stakes negotiations after the criminal's brilliant heist spirals into a hostage situation. **Fun Fact:** The scene in the coffee shop was improvised. On the DVD commentary, Spike Lee states that when Denzel Washington ad-libbed the line "I'll bet you can get a cab though," he nearly ruined the take by laughing so loud at Washington's line.

☐ **The Italian Job (1969):** Comic caper movie about a plan to steal a gold shipment from the streets of Turin by creating a traffic jam.

☐ **Joker (2019):** In Gotham City, mentally troubled comedian Arthur Fleck is disregarded and mistreated by society. He then embarks on a downward spiral of revolution and bloody crime. This path brings him face-to-face with his alter-ego: The Joker. **Memorable Quote:** *"The worst part of having a mental illness is people expect you to behave as if you don't."*

☐ **The Killing (1956):** Crook Johnny Clay assembles a five-man team to plan and execute a daring racetrack robbery.

☐ **Knives Out (2019):** A detective investigates the death of a patriarch of an eccentric, combative family. **Fun Fact:** Both the title "Knives Out" and the working title "Morning Bell" are tracks from the album *Amnesiac* (2001) by the English rock band Radiohead.

☐ **L.A. Confidential (1997):** As corruption grows in 1950s Los Angeles, three policemen -- one strait-laced, one brutally tough and one sleazy -- investigate a series of murders with their own brand of justice.

☐ **The Lady Vanishes (1938):** While travelling in continental Europe, a rich young playgirl realizes that an elderly lady seems to have disappeared from the train. **Goof:** In Europe, the hotel manager says it is "spring" when talking about the avalanches. However, the two English travelers are trying to get back to England for the Manchester cricket test, which was always played in July.

☐ **Laura (1944):** A police detective falls in love with the woman whose murder he is investigating.

☐ **Lock, Stock and Two Smoking Barrels (1998):** Eddy persuades his three pals to pool money for a vital poker game against a powerful local mobster, Hatchet Harry. Eddy loses, after which Harry gives him a week to pay back 500,000 pounds. **Fun Fact:** This was Jason Statham's film debut.

☐ **The Maltese Falcon (1941):** A private detective takes on a case that involves him with three eccentric criminals, a gorgeous liar and their quest for a priceless statuette. **Memorable Quote:** *"The stuff that dreams are made of."*

☐ **The Manchurian Candidate (1962):** A former prisoner of war is brainwashed as an unwitting assassin for an international Communist conspiracy.

☐ **Mean Streets (1973):** A small-time hood tries to keep the peace between his friend Johnny and Johnny's creditors. **Fun Fact:** Francis Ford Coppola contributed money to the budget of the film.

☐ **Miller's Crossing (1990):** Tom Reagan, an advisor to a Prohibition-era crime boss, tries to keep the peace between warring mobs but gets caught in divided loyalties.

- [ ] **Memento (2000):** A man with short-term memory loss attempts to track down his wife's murderer.

- [ ] **Nightcrawler (2014):** When Louis Bloom, a con man desperate for work, muscles into the world of L.A. crime journalism, he blurs the line between observer and participant to become the star of his own story. **Fun Fact:** During the scene where Jake Gyllenhaal screams at himself in the mirror, Gyllenhaal got so into the scene that the mirror cracked, cutting his hand. He had to go to the hospital for 14 stitches, returning to the set after being discharged.

- [ ] **The Night of the Hunter (1955):** A religious fanatic marries a gullible widow whose young children are reluctant to tell him where their real daddy hid the $10,000 he'd stolen in a robbery. **Goof:** While in prison for a misdemeanor, Harry Powell shares a cell with a death row inmate, who mutters in his sleep about a stolen fortune. In real life, a man charged with a misdemeanor wouldn't be in the same facility as a death row inmate, let alone the same cell.

- [ ] **Nocturnal Animals (2016):** A wealthy art gallery owner is haunted by her ex-husband's novel, a violent thriller she interprets as a symbolic revenge tale. **Fun Fact:** Although he is known as a fashion designer, director Tom Ford chose to leave the costuming in the film strictly to the costume designer. Not a single Tom Ford product appears in the film, as Ford "didn't want a commercial."

- [ ] **Point Break (1991):** An F.B.I. Agent goes undercover to catch a gang of surfers who may be bank robbers.

- [ ] **Prisoners (2013):** When Keller Dover's daughter and her friend go missing, he takes matters into his own hands as the police pursue multiple leads and the pressure mounts. **Goof:** When Keller is deer hunting with his son, the two families are celebrating Thanksgiving. The film takes place in Pennsylvania, where deer hunting season does not begin until the first Monday after Thanksgiving.

☐ **Rear Window (1954):** A wheelchair-bound photographer spies on his neighbors from his apartment window and becomes convinced one of them has committed murder. **Goof:** Alfred Hitchcock was a master of suspense, but not necessarily a master of common sense. In this taut thriller, James Stewart's character is a professional photojournalist who is armed with a high-powered camera and a boatload of suspicions about his neighbor. And yet he never takes a single photo of the neighbor's potential misdeeds.

☐ **Reservoir Dogs (1992);** When a simple jewelry heist goes horribly wrong, the surviving criminals begin to suspect that one of them is a police informant. **Fun Fact:** James Woods fired his agent upon learning – after the movie was shot – that Quentin Tarantino wanted him for a part in *Reservoir Dogs*.

☐ **Scarface (1983):** In 1980 Miami, a determined Cuban immigrant takes over a drug cartel and succumbs to greed. **My Favorite Line:** *"Say Hello to my little friend."*

☐ **Serpico (1973):** An honest New York cop named Frank Serpico blows the whistle on rampant corruption in the force only to have his comrades turn against him.

☐ **Se7en (1995):** Two detectives, a rookie and a veteran, hunt a serial killer who uses the seven deadly sins as his motives. **Fun Fact:** As preparation for his traumatic scene in the interrogation room, Leland Orser would breathe in and out rapidly, so that his body would be overly saturated with oxygen, giving him the ability to hyperventilate. He also did not sleep for a few days, in order to achieve his character's disoriented look.

☐ **Shadow of a Doubt (1943):** A young girl, overjoyed when her favorite uncle comes to visit the family, slowly begins to suspect that he is in fact the "Merry Widow" killer sought by the authorities.

☐ **Shutter Island (2010):** In 1954, a U.S. Marshal investigates the disappearance of a murderer who escaped from a hospital for the criminally insane. **Goof:** The film is set in the Boston harbor area however the geography is clearly that of the Pacific coast. The island is steep and rocky with predominant black volcanic rock especially in the bluff scenes.

☐ **Split (2016):** Three girls are kidnapped by a man with a diagnosed 23 distinct personalities. They must try to escape before the apparent emergence of a frightful new 24th.

☐ **Strangers on a Train (1951):** A psychopath forces a tennis star to comply with his theory that two strangers can get away with murder. **Fun Fact:** The stunt where the man crawled under the carousel was not done with trick photography. Alfred Hitchcock claimed that this was the most dangerous stunt ever performed under his direction, and he would never allow it to be done again.

☐ **Taxi Driver (1976):** A mentally unstable veteran works as a nighttime taxi driver in New York City, where the perceived decadence and sleaze fuels his urge for violent action by attempting to liberate a presidential campaign worker and an underage prostitute. **Fun Fact:** Paul Schrader wrote *Taxi Driver* in five days. It is rumored he had a loaded gun by his desk for "inspiration and motivation." **My Favorite Line:** *"You talking to me?"*

☐ **The Third Man (1949):** Pulp novelist Holly Martins travels to shadowy, postwar Vienna, only to find himself investigating the mysterious death of an old friend, Harry Lime. **Goof:** In Joseph Cotton and Orson Wells' first scene together, Cotton yells out his famous line "What kind of spy do you think you are, satchel foot?" but his mouth clearly isn't moving.

☐ **The Thomas Crown Affair (1968):** A debonair, adventuresome bank executive believes he has pulled off the perfect multi-million-dollar heist, only to match wits with a sexy insurance investigator who will do anything to get her man.

☐ **Touch of Evil (1958):** A stark, perverse story of murder, kidnapping, and police corruption in a Mexican border town. **Goof:** This noirish thriller from Orson Welles opens with one of the most emblematic long shots in cinematic history. At the beginning of the famously extended sequence, a crew member is briefly visible in the upper left-hand corner of the screen.

- ☐ **The Untouchables (1987):** During the era of Prohibition in the United States, Federal Agent Eliot Ness sets out to stop ruthless Chicago gangster Al Capone and, because of rampant corruption, assembles a small, hand-picked team to help him.

- ☐ **Witness for the Prosecution (1957):** A veteran British barrister must defend his client in a murder trial that has surprise after surprise. **Memorable Quote:** *"The question is, Frau Helm, were you lying then, are you lying now, or are you not in fact a chronic and habitual LIAR!"*

Cult Classics

How do you define a cult classic? Films that are so, so bad, they are good? Films that didn't get the recognition they deserved? Quotable movies? Critic-hated films but were loved by the masses? All correct.

According to Wikipedia, a **cult film** or **cult movie**, also commonly referred to as a **cult classic**, is a film that has acquired a cult following. Cult films are known for their dedicated, passionate fanbase which forms an elaborate subculture, members of which engage in repeated viewings, dialogue-quoting, and audience participation. Inclusive definitions allow for major studio productions, especially box office bombs, while exclusive definitions focus more on obscure, transgressive films shunned by the mainstream. The difficulty in defining the term and subjectivity of what qualifies as a cult film mirror classificatory disputes about art. The term *cult film* itself was first used in the 1970s to describe the culture that surrounded underground films and midnight movies, though *cult* was in common use in film analysis for decades prior to that.

Cult films trace their origin back to controversial and suppressed films kept alive by dedicated fans. In some cases, reclaimed or rediscovered films have acquired cult followings decades after their original release, occasionally for their camp value. Other cult films have since become well-respected or reassessed as classics; there is debate as to whether these popular and accepted films are still cult films. After failing in the cinema, some cult films have become regular fixtures on cable television or profitable sellers on home video. Others have inspired their own film festivals. Cult films can both appeal to specific subcultures and form their own subcultures. Other media that reference cult films can easily identify which demographics they desire to attract and offer savvy fans an opportunity to demonstrate their knowledge.

Cult films frequently break cultural taboos, and many feature excessive displays of violence, gore, sexuality, profanity, or combinations thereof. This can lead to controversy, censorship, and outright bans; less transgressive films may attract similar amounts of controversy when critics call them frivolous or incompetent. Films that fail to attract requisite amounts of controversy may face resistance when labeled as cult films. Mainstream films and big budget blockbusters have attracted cult followings similar to more underground and lesser-known films; fans of these films often emphasize the films' niche appeal and reject the more popular aspects. Fans who like the films for the wrong reasons, such as perceived elements that represent mainstream appeal and marketing, will often be ostracized or ridiculed. Likewise, fans who stray from accepted subcultural scripts may experience similar rejection.

Since the late 1970s, cult films have become increasingly popular. Films that once would have been limited to obscure cult followings are now capable of breaking into the mainstream, and showings of cult films have proved to be a profitable business venture. Overbroad usage of the term has resulted in controversy, as purists state it has become a meaningless descriptor applied to any film that is the slightest bit weird or unconventional; others accuse Hollywood studios of trying to artificially create cult films or use the term as a marketing tactic. Films are frequently stated to be an "instant cult classic" now, occasionally before they are released. Fickle fans on the Internet have latched on to unreleased films only to abandon them later on release. At the same time, other films have acquired massive, quick cult followings, owing to spreading virally through social media. Easy access to cult films via video on demand and peer-to-peer file sharing has led some critics to pronounce the death of cult films.

☐ **American Psycho (2000):** A wealthy New York City investment banking executive, Patrick Bateman, hides his alternate psychopathic ego from his co-workers and friends as he delves deeper into his violent, hedonistic fantasies. **Fun Fact:** Christian Bale drew inspiration from Tom Cruise for his character stating, "very intense friendliness with nothing behind the eyes."

☐ **Army of Darkness (1992):** A sardonic hardware store clerk is accidentally transported to 1300 A.D., where he must retrieve the Necronomicon and battle an army of the dead so he can return home.

☐ **Attack of the Killer Tomatoes! (1978):** A group of scientists band together to save the world from mutated killer tomatoes.

☐ **Being John Malkovich (1999):** A puppeteer discovers a portal that leads literally into the head of movie star John Malkovich. **Goof:** Pressing "emergency stop" on an elevator wouldn't set off any alarms. It might alert security but one would have to hit the alarm button to sound an alarm.

☐ **Big Trouble in Little China (1986):** A rough-and-tumble trucker helps rescue his friend's fiancée from an ancient sorcerer in a supernatural battle beneath Chinatown.

☐ **Clerks (1994):** A day in the lives of two convenience clerks named Dante and Randal as they annoy customers, discuss movies, and play hockey on the store roof. **Fun Fact:** Kevin Smith, a keen comic book fan, sold a large part of his collection to help fund this film. He has since been able to buy most of them back.

☐ **Death Becomes Her (1992):** When a woman learns of an immortality treatment, she sees it as a way to outdo her long-time rival.

☐ **Dazed and Confused (1993):** The adventures of high school and junior high students on the last day of school in May 1976. **My Favorite Line:** *"All right, all right, all right."*

☐ **Donnie Darko (2001):** After narrowly escaping a bizarre accident, a troubled teenager is plagued by visions of a man in a large rabbit suit who manipulates him to commit a series of crimes.

☐ **Earth Girls are Easy (1988):** A Southern California girl befriends three furry aliens after their spaceship lands in her swimming pool. **Best Song in the Entire World:** "Because I'm a Blonde."

☐ **Empire Records (1995):** Twenty-four hours in the lives of the young employees at Empire Records when they all grow up and become young adults thanks to each other and the manager. They all face the store joining a chain store with strict rules.

☐ **Escape from New York (1981):** In 1997, when the U.S. president crashes into Manhattan, now a giant maximum-security prison, a convicted bank robber is sent in to rescue him. **Fun Fact:** Kurt Russell has stated that this is his favorite of all his films, and Snake Plissken is his favorite of his characters.

☐ **Event Horizon (1997):** A rescue crew investigates a spaceship that disappeared into a black hole and has now returned...with someone or something new on-board.

☐ **Fear and Loathing in Las Vegas (1998):** An oddball journalist and his psychopathic lawyer travel to Las Vegas for a series of psychedelic escapades. **Fun Fact:** In the book, Hunter S. Thompson listens to "Sympathy for the Devil" by The Rolling Stones. The rights to play it in the film were too expensive for the production's budget.

☐ **Fight Club (1999):** An insomniac office worker and a devil-may-care soap maker form an underground fight club that evolves into something much, much more. **Fun Fact:** Brad Pitt and Edward Norton both really learned how to make soap. **Fun Fact:** Marla Singer's line of "I haven't been fucked like that since grade school" in *Fight Club* was an alternative to the line "I want to have your abortion." Head of Fox 2000, Laura Ziskin, said David Fincher could have any line but the original. Hating the new line even more, she still stood by her promise. **Memorable Quote:** *"The first rule of Fight Club is: You do not talk about Fight Club."*

☐ **Fire Walk with Me (1992):** Laura Palmer's harrowing final days are chronicled one year after the murder of Teresa Banks, a resident of Twin Peaks' neighboring town.

☐ **Friday (1995):** It's Friday, and Craig and Smokey must come up with $200 they owe a local bully or there won't be a Saturday. **My Favorite Line:** *"Bye, Felisha."* **Side Note:** That's how it is spelled in the cast listing.

☐ **Ghost World (2001):** With only the plan of moving in together after high school, two unusually devious friends seek direction in life. As a mere gag, they respond to a man's newspaper ad for a date, only to find it will greatly complicate their lives.

☐ **Harold and Maude (1971):** Young, rich, and obsessed with death, Harold finds himself changed forever when he meets lively septuagenarian Maude at a funeral. **Fun Fact:** In all shots of Ruth Gordon (Maude) driving the hearse it is being towed because she never learned how to drive a car.

☐ **Hedwig and the Angry Inch (2001):** A gender-queer punk-rock singer from East Berlin tours the U.S. with her band as she tells her life story and follows the former lover/band-mate who stole her songs.

☐ **Idiocracy (2006):** Private Joe Bauers, a decisively average American, is selected as a guinea pig for a top-secret hibernation program but is forgotten, awakening to a future so incredibly moronic he's easily the most intelligent person alive. **Memorable Quote:** *"The #1 movie in America was called "Ass." And that's all it was for 90 minutes. It won eight Oscars that year, including best screenplay."*

☐ **Jawbreaker (1999):** Three of the most popular girls at Reagan High accidentally kill the prom queen with a jawbreaker when a kidnapping goes horribly wrong.

☐ **Kids (1995):** A day in the life of a group of teens as they travel around New York City skating, drinking, smoking and deflowering virgins. **Fun Fact:** The film received an NC-17 rating from the MPAA (no one under 18 admitted). Clark appealed the rating, and lost. The MPAA recommend that Clark not cut the film because they felt it would lose some of its impact.

☐ **Labyrinth (1986):** Sixteen-year-old Sarah is given thirteen hours to solve a labyrinth and rescue her baby brother Toby when her wish for him to be taken away is granted by the Goblin King Jareth.

☐ **The Man Who Fell to Earth (1976):** An alien must pose as a human to save his dying planet, but a woman and greed of other men create complications.

☐ **Office Space (1999):** Three company workers who hate their jobs decide to rebel against their greedy boss. **Memorable Quote:** *"Uh oh. Sounds like somebody's got a case of the Mondays."* **My Favorite Line:** *"I believe you have my stapler."*

☐ **Pi (1998):** A paranoid mathematician searches for a key number that will unlock the universal patterns found in nature.

☐ **The Princess Bride (1987):** While home sick in bed, a young boy's grandfather reads him the story of a farmboy-turned-pirate who encounters numerous obstacles in his quest to be reunited with his true love. **Memorable Quote:** *"Hello. My name is Inigo Montoya. You killed my father. Prepare to die."*

☐ **The Raid (2011):** A S.W.A.T. team becomes trapped in a tenement run by a ruthless mobster and his army of killers and thugs.

☐ **Real Genius (1985):** Teenage geniuses deal with their abilities while developing a high-powered laser for a university project. When their professor intends to turn their work into a military weapon, they decide to ruin his plans. **Fun Fact:** When Lazlo Hollyfeld sends in a large number of entries to the Frito-Lay contest, he is mirroring the actions of Caltech students Steve Klein, Dave Novikoff and Barry Megdal, who, in 1974, used a similar strategy to win a McDonald's sweepstakes. Their entries came to roughly 1/5th of the total entries and won them a station wagon, $3,000 cash and $1,500 in food gift certificates.

☐ **Reefer Madness (2005):** An outrageous tongue-in-cheek musical comedy adaptation of the classic anti-marijuana propaganda film Reefer Madness (1936).

☐ **Repo Man (1984):** A young punk recruited by a car repossession agency finds himself in pursuit of a Chevrolet Malibu that is wanted for a $20,000 bounty - and has something otherworldly stashed in its trunk. **Goof:** License plate on the Malibu. There are no front plates in New Mexico

☐ **Repo! The Genetic Opera (2008):** A young punk recruited by a car repossession agency finds himself in pursuit of a Chevrolet Malibu that is wanted for a $20,000 bounty - and has something otherworldly stashed in its trunk.

☐ **Requiem for a Dream (2000):** The drug-induced utopias of four Coney Island people are shattered when their addictions run deep. **Fun Fact:** Darren Aronofsky shot the film like a hip-hop montage (a sequence of extremely short shots) to get the sense of overwhelming addiction and loss of control. An average 100-minute film contains 600 to 700 cuts; this one contains over 2,000.

☐ **The Room (2003):** Johnny is a successful bank executive who lives quietly in a San Francisco townhouse with his fiancée, Lisa. One day, putting aside any scruple, she seduces Johnny's best friend, Mark. From there, nothing will be the same again. **My Two Cents:** This is one of those so bad, it could possibly be good movies. Like I think this is the worst movie on the list.

☐ **The Royal Tenenbaums (2001):** The eccentric members of a dysfunctional family reluctantly gather under the same roof for various reasons. **Memorable Quote:** "*I'm very sorry for your loss. Your mother was a terribly attractive woman.*"

☐ **Rushmore (1998):** The extracurricular king of Rushmore Preparatory School is put on academic probation.

☐ **Shaft (2000):** New York City police detective John Shaft (nephew of the original 1970s detective) goes on a personal mission to make sure the son of a real estate tycoon is brought to justice after a racially-motivated murder.

☐ **Show Girls (1995):** Nomi, a young drifter, arrives in Las Vegas to become a dancer and soon sets about clawing and pushing her way to become the top of the Vegas showgirls. **Fun Fact:** *Showgirls* still holds the record for most Razzie (anti-Oscars) nominations with 13.

Paul Verhoeven was the first director to collect the award for Worst Picture in person.

- ☐ **Singles (1992):** A group of twenty-something friends, most of whom live in the same apartment complex, search for love and success in grunge-era Seattle.

- ☐ **Slap Shot (1977):** A failing ice hockey team finds success with outrageously violent hockey gooney. **Goof:** During the championship game, cardboard cutouts to fill in the "crowd" can be clearly seen in the upper levels of the arena.

- ☐ **Spaceballs (1987):** A star-pilot for hire and his trusty sidekick must come to the rescue of a princess and save Planet Druidia from the clutches of the evil Spaceballs.

- ☐ **Stranger than Paradise (1984):** A New Yorker's life is thrown into a tailspin when his younger cousin surprise-visits him, starting a strange, unpredictable adventure. **Fun Fact:** The film's scenes are each a single shot, followed by a few seconds of black screen.

- ☐ **Super Troopers (2001):** Five Vermont state troopers, avid pranksters with a knack for screwing up, try to save their jobs and out-do the local police department by solving a crime.

- ☐ **To Wong Foo Thanks for Everything, Julie Newmar (1995):** Three drag queens travel cross-country until their car breaks down, leaving them stranded in a small town. **Memorable Quote:** *"When a lady says no, she means... get your hand off my dick, buddy!"*

- ☐ **Up in Smoke (1978):** Two stoners unknowingly smuggle a van - made entirely of marijuana - from Mexico to L.A., with incompetent Sgt. Stedenko on their trail.

- ☐ **Valley of the Dolls (1967):** Film version of Jacqueline Susann's best-selling novel chronicling the rise and fall of three young women in show business. **Fun Fact:** Judy Garland was originally cast in the role of Helen Lawson. She was fired because of her drinking and behavior and was replaced by Susan Hayward. Other actors considered as replacements were Tammy Grimes and Bette Davis.

☐ **Waiting… (2005):** Film version of Jacqueline Susann's best-selling novel chronicling the rise and fall of three young women in show business. **Memorable Quote:** *"You know, we should probably feel guilty, but she broke the cardinal rule: Don't fuck with people that handle your food."* **Side Note:** Don't EVER send food back, they will fuck with your food. ALWAYS! Yes, ALWAYS!

☐ **The Warriors (1979):** In the near future, a charismatic leader summons the street gangs of New York City in a bid to take it over. When he is killed, The Warriors are falsely blamed and now must fight their way home while every other gang is hunting them down.

☐ **Welcome to the Dollhouse (1995):** An awkward seventh-grader struggles to cope with inattentive parents, snobbish class-mates, a smart older brother, an attractive younger sister and her own insecurities in suburban New Jersey.

☐ **Wet Hot American Summer (2001):** Set on the last day of camp, in the hot summer of 1981, a group of counselors try to complete their unfinished business before the day ends. **Fun Fact:** The owners of Camp Towanda (where the movie was filmed) were told that this was going to be a family comedy. They were mortified when they saw the final cut of the film.

☐ **The Wiz (1978):** An adaptation of "The Wizard of Oz" that tries to capture the essence of the African-American experience.

☐ **Withnail & I (1987):** In 1969, two substance-abusing, unemployed actors retreat to the countryside for a holiday that proves disastrous. **Memorable Quote:** *"I feel like a pig shat in my head."*

Disney Films

I am sure all of these are free in the Disney app subscription, that is why there is no "Free" bold section. If it is free on a different app or website I will put it, but, again, I doubt it. I included old Disney classics I remembered as a child because I like reminiscing. Also, Disney cartoons like to reference sexual connotations a lot. I have listed the ones I know.

☐ **Aladdin (1992):** A kindhearted street urchin and a power-hungry Grand Vizier vie for a magic lamp that has the power to make their deepest wishes come true. **Fun Fact:** When Aladdin goes off the balcony, you can hear a whisper that says "Take off your clothes."

☐ **Alice in Wonderland (1951):** Alice stumbles into the world of Wonderland. Will she get home? Not if the Queen of Hearts has her way.

☐ **The Apple Dumpling Gang (1975):** Three orphan children strike gold in 1878 California. **Goof:** When the earthquake occurs while the children are in the mine, the Earth is shown splitting open. During an earthquake, the fault sides slide past each other, they do not split apart. Splitting apart is something only seen in the movies.

☐ **Babes in Toyland (1961):** Mary Contrary is set to marry Tom Piper when he is kidnapped by Roderigo and Gonzorgo, two goons working for the evil Barnaby who wants to marry Mary for her inheritance.

☐ **Bambi (1942):** The story of a young deer growing up in the forest. **Memorable Quote:** *"Eating greens is a special treat, it makes long ears and great big feet. But it sure is awful stuff to eat." I made that last part up myself."*

☐ **Beauty and the Beast (1991):** A prince cursed to spend his days as a hideous monster sets out to regain his humanity by earning a young woman's love.

☐ **Big Hero 6 (2014):** A special bond develops between plus-sized inflatable robot Baymax and prodigy Hiro Hamada, who together team up with a group of friends to form a band of high-tech heroes. **Fun Facts:** The production team watched videos of fire ants as an inspiration of the movement of the Microbots.

☐ **Blackbeard's Ghost (1968):** On the Carolina coast, Godolphin College's new track coach lodges at Blackbeard's Inn, run by the daughters of the Buccaneers, who claim to be descendants of the notorious pirate, and who risk losing their hotel to the local mobster.

☐ **Brave (2012):** Determined to make her own path in life, Princess Merida (Kelly Macdonald) defies a custom that brings chaos to her kingdom. Granted one wish, Merida must rely on her bravery and her archery skills to undo a beastly curse. **Memorable Quote:** *"There are those who say fate is something beyond our command. That destiny is not our own, but I know better. Our fate lives within us, you only have to be brave enough to see it."*

☐ **Camp Nowhere (1994):** A group of junior high kids don't want to go to summer camps chosen by their parents. They make their own adult-free camp and "hire" an ex-drama teacher to help.

☐ **Cinderella (1950):** When Cinderella's cruel stepmother prevents her from attending the Royal Ball, she gets some unexpected help from the lovable mice Gus and Jaq, and from her Fairy Godmother. **Fun Fact:** Watch the scene where the mice steal the beads as an adult.

☐ **Coco (2017):** Aspiring musician Miguel, confronted with his family's ancestral ban on music, enters the Land of the Dead to find his great-great-grandfather, a legendary singer.

☐ **Darby O'Gill and the Little People (1959):** A wily old codger matches wits with the King of the Leprechauns and helps play matchmaker for his daughter and the strapping lad who has replaced him as caretaker.

☐ **Dumbo (1941):** Ridiculed because of his enormous ears, a young circus elephant is assisted by a mouse to achieve his full potential. **Goof:** Dumbo drinks the beer through his trunk rather than spraying it into his mouth.

☐ **Escape to Witch Mountain (1975):** Two mysterious orphan children have extraordinary powers and are chased by a scheming millionaire. But where do these kids really call home?

☐ **Fantasia (1940):** A collection of animated interpretations of great works of Western classical music. **Fun Fact:** During production, the animators were given no instructions for coloring. Walt Disney instructed them to use any colors they wanted--a first.

☐ **Finding Nemo (2003):** After his son is captured in the Great Barrier Reef and taken to Sydney, a timid clownfish sets out on a journey to bring him home.

☐ **Frozen (2013):** When the newly crowned Queen Elsa accidentally uses her power to turn things into ice to curse her home in infinite winter, her sister Anna teams up with a mountain man, his playful reindeer, and a snowman to change the weather condition. **Fun Fact:** Did you miss the joke about "foot size?"

☐ **Hercules (1997):** The son of Zeus and Hera is stripped of his immortality as an infant and must become a true hero in order to reclaim it.

☐ **Holes (2003):** A wrongfully convicted boy is sent to a brutal desert detention camp where he joins the job of digging holes for some mysterious reason. **Memorable Quote:** *"I'm not stupid, I know everyone thinks I am, I just don't like answering stupid questions."*

☐ **Honey, I Shrunk the Kids (1989):** The scientist father of a teenage girl and boy accidentally shrinks his and two other neighborhood teens to the size of insects. Now the teens must fight diminutive dangers as the father searches for them.

☐ **The Hunchback of Notre Dame (1996):** A deformed bell-ringer must assert his independence from a vicious government minister in order to help his friend, a gypsy dancer. **Fun Fact:** You can see the naked body of Esmerelda through the flames.

☐ **The Incredibles (2004):** A family of undercover superheroes, while trying to live the quiet suburban life, are forced into action to save the world.

☐ **The Jungle Book (1967):** Bagheera the Panther and Baloo the Bear have a difficult time trying to convince a boy to leave the jungle for human civilization. **Goof:** The story takes place in India, yet King Louie is an orangutan - they live in Borneo and Sumatra. Disney's promotional materials later solved this problem by declaring that Louie is an undiscovered "cryptid" species, which is also mentioned in *The Jungle Book* (2016).

☐ **Lady and the Tramp (1955):** The romantic tale of a sheltered uptown Cocker Spaniel dog and a streetwise downtown Mutt.

☐ **Lilo and Stitch (2002):** A young and parentless girl adopts a 'dog' from the local pound, completely unaware that it's supposedly a dangerous scientific experiment that's taken refuge on Earth and is now hiding from its creator and those who see it as a menace. **Crazy Credit:** One of the photos of Nani, Lilo, Stitch, et al. displayed at the end has them posing at the gate of Graceland, continuing the story of Lilo and Stitch's love of the music and style of Elvis Presley.

☐ **The Lion King (1994):** Lion prince Simba and his father are targeted by his bitter uncle, who wants to ascend the throne himself. **Fun Fact:** When Simba lays down and the dust flies, it spells "SEX."

☐ **The Little Mermaid (1989):** A mermaid princess makes a Faustian bargain in an attempt to become human and win a prince's love. **Fun Fact:** In the original movie poster, the top of the castle was a penis head.

☐ **The Love Bug (1968):** A race car driver becomes a champion with a Volkswagen Beetle with a mind of its own.

☐ **Mary Poppins (1964):** In turn of the century London, a magical nanny employs music and adventure to help two neglected children become closer to their father. **Best Song:** "Chim-Chim-Cheree." **Side Note:** I made parody of this song about Hollywood. I may try to release it someday.

☐ **Mighty Joe Young (1998):** A legendary fifteen-foot-tall mountain gorilla named Joe is taken to an animal sanctuary in California by zoologist Gregg O'Hara and Jill Young, with whom he grew up. Poacher Strasser returns from the past to seek vengeance on Joe.

☐ **Moana (2016):** In Ancient Polynesia, when a terrible curse incurred by the Demigod Maui reaches Moana's island, she answers the Ocean's call to seek out the Demigod to set things right. **Goof:** The movie features several frigate birds, particularly when baby Moana helps the baby turtle get to the sea. Polynesians sometimes used frigate birds to help navigate toward new islands. However, they spend very little time on land, and never eat there. They hunt while in flight in the open sea, and only land when they need to roost.

☐ **Monsters, Inc. (2001):** In order to power the city, monsters have to scare children so that they scream. However, the children are toxic to the monsters, and after a child gets through, two monsters realize things may not be what they think.

☐ **Mulan (1998):** To save her father from death in the army, a young maiden secretly goes in his place and becomes one of China's greatest heroines in the process. **My Two Cents:** My nickname in high school was Mulan, because the study hall teacher repeatedly mispronounced my name and all the seniors thought it was hilarious when I was a freshman.

☐ **The Nightmare Before Christmas (1993):** Jack Skellington, king of Halloween Town, discovers Christmas Town, but his attempts to bring Christmas to his home causes confusion.

☐ **Old Yeller (1957):** A teenage boy grows to love a stray yellow dog while helping his mother and younger brother run their Texas homestead while their father is away on a cattle drive. First thought to be good-for-nothing mutt, Old Yeller is soon beloved by all. **Memorable Quote:** *"Now and then, for no good reason a man can figure out, life will just haul off and knock him flat."*

☐ **One Hundred and One Dalmatians (1961):** When a litter of Dalmatian puppies are abducted by the minions of Cruella De Vil, the parents must find them before she uses them for a diabolical fashion statement. **Goof:** The puppies have American accents, even though the film is set in England and their parents and owners (and indeed virtually every other character) have English accents.

☐ **Operation Dumbo Drop (1995):** To keep the loyalty of a village during the Vietnam war, a U.S. Army officer and his unit struggle to deliver it a live elephant.

☐ **The Parent Trap (1961):** Teenage twin sisters swap places and scheme to reunite their divorced parents. If you want to count the Lindsay Lohan remake, I guess that would be ok. **Fun Fact:** Joanna Barnes (Vicky Robinson) is the only actress to also appear in *The Parent Trap* (1998). She plays an older version of her character, who has passed her gold-digging ways on to her daughter Meredith.

☐ **Peter Pan (1953):** Wendy and her brothers are whisked away to the magical world of Neverland with the hero of their stories, Peter Pan.

☐ **Ratatouille (2007):** A rat who can cook makes an unusual alliance with a young kitchen worker at a famous restaurant. **Fun Fact:** Look for all the sex jokes such as vegetable as sex toys, and having a small wiener.

☐ **The Shaggy Dog (1959):** A teenage boy is cursed with periodically turning into a sheepdog.

☐ **Snow White and the Seven Dwarves (1937):** Exiled into the dangerous forest by her wicked stepmother, a princess is rescued by seven dwarf miners who make her part of their household. **Misquote:** "Mirror, mirror, on the wall, who is the fairest of them all?" **Actual quote:** "Magic mirror, on the wall, who is the fairest *one of all*?"

☐ **Swiss Family Robinson (1960):** A Swiss family must survive being shipwrecked on a deserted island.

☐ **Tall Tale (1995):** A young boy's imagination summons cowboy legend Pecos Bill, who helps him save the family farm from a greedy land-grabber. With the help of a lumberjack and a railroad worker, they all embark on a surprise-filled adventure. I feel like this was one of my favorite movies as a kid. It's probably because I had a crush on the main character.

☐ **Toy Story Franchise (1995):** A cowboy doll is profoundly threatened and jealous when a new spaceman figure supplants him as top toy in a boy's room. **Fun Fact:** In Sid's room he has a "Hooker" toy. It's a fishing hook with Barbie doll legs. **Memorable Quotes:** *"To infinity and beyond!"*

☐ **Up (2009):** 78-year-old Carl Fredricksen travels to Paradise Falls in his house equipped with balloons, inadvertently taking a young stowaway. **Fun Fact:** There were 10,297 balloons in *Up*.

☐ **Wall-E (2008):** In the distant future, a small waste-collecting robot inadvertently embarks on a space journey that will ultimately decide the fate of mankind.

☐ **Who Framed Roger Rabbit (1988):** A toon-hating detective is a cartoon rabbit's only hope to prove his innocence when he is accused of murder. **Fun Fact:** As Jessica Rabbit is thrown from the car, she exposes herself.

☐ **Wild Hearts Can't be Broken (1991):** Thrilled by a performance she sees at a fair, Sonora tries to land a spot as a daredevil who rides horses off of high dives.

Drama

This list is smaller than the rest as I feel most of the dramas have already been stated in the Academy Awards section. So, I have kept this short and sweet.

☐ **About Time (2013):** At the age of 21, Tim discovers he can travel in time and change what happens and has happened in his own life. His decision to make his world a better place by getting a girlfriend turns out not to be as easy as you might think.

☐ **American History X (1998):** A former neo-Nazi skinhead tries to prevent his younger brother from going down the same wrong path that he did. **Fun Fact:** Before filming began, Edward Norton and Edward Furlong shaved their heads for their roles. Edward Norton also gained 30 pounds of muscle.

☐ **Big Fish (2003):** A frustrated son tries to determine the fact from fiction in his dying father's life.

☐ **Casino (1995):** A tale of greed, deception, money, power, and murder occur between two best friends: a mafia enforcer and a casino executive compete against each other over a gambling empire, and over a fast-living and fast-loving socialite.

☐ **Citizen Kane (1941):** Following the death of publishing tycoon Charles Foster Kane, reporters scramble to uncover the meaning of his final utterance: 'Rosebud'. **Fun Fact:** Orson Welles directed much of *Citizen Kane* from a wheelchair, after injuring himself on set. **Goof:** The most famous word ever spoken on film might very well be "rosebud," uttered by Charles Foster Kane before he takes his final breath. As reporters scramble to figure out the meaning behind the word, some viewers might wonder how those reporters heard it in the first place, as Kane appeared to be alone when he died. The most ardent fans argue there was a butler in the room, but to this day it remains unclear.

☐ **The Color Purple (1985):** An African-American woman struggles to find her identity after suffering abuse from her father.

☐ **Cool Hand Luke (1967):** A laid back Southern man is sentenced to two years in a rural prison, but refuses to conform.

☐ **Dead Man Walking (1995):** A nun, while comforting a convicted killer on death row, empathizes with both the killer and his victim's families. **Goof:** The chemicals used in lethal injections in Louisiana are administered manually, not by a machine as in the movie.

☐ **Do the Right Thing (1989):** On the hottest day of the year on a street in the Bedford-Stuyvesant section of Brooklyn, everyone's hate and bigotry smolders and builds until it explodes into violence.

☐ **The Father (2020):** A man refuses all assistance from his daughter as he ages. As he tries to make sense of his changing circumstances, he begins to doubt his loved ones, his own mind and even the fabric of his reality. **Memorable Quote:** *"I feel as if I'm losing my all leaves..."*

☐ **Glengarry, Glen Ross (1992):** An examination of the machinations behind the scenes at a real estate office.

☐ **The Graduate (1967):** A disillusioned graduate finds himself torn between his older lover and her daughter. **Misquote:** "Mrs. Robinson, are you trying to seduce me?" **Actual Quote:** "Mrs. Robinson, *you're trying* to seduce me, *aren't you*?"

☐ **Gran Torino (2008):** Disgruntled Korean War veteran Walt Kowalski sets out to reform his neighbor, Thao Lor, a Hmong teenager who tried to steal Kowalski's prized possession: a 1972 Gran Torino.

☐ **The Green Mile (1999):** The lives of guards on Death Row are affected by one of their charges: a black man accused of child murder and rape, yet who has a mysterious gift.

☐ **Jeff, Who Lives at Home (2011):** Dispatched from his basement room on an errand for his widowed mother, slacker Jeff might discover his destiny (finally) when he spends the day with his unhappily married brother as he tracks his possibly adulterous wife. **My Two Cents:** Again, this is one of my picks just because of how I believe the world works. You might not understand at the moment but it comes together in the end.

☐ **To Kill a Mockingbird (1962):** Atticus Finch, a lawyer in the Depression-era South, defends a black man against an undeserved rape charge, and his children against prejudice.

☐ **The Last Picture Show (1971):** In 1951, a group of high schoolers come of age in a bleak, isolated, atrophied North Texas town that is slowly dying, both culturally and economically. **Memorable Quote:** *"Never you mind, honey. Never you mind."*

☐ **Letter from an Unknown Woman (1948):** A pianist about to flee from a duel receives a letter from a woman he cannot remember, who may hold the key to his downfall.

☐ **Life as a House (2001):** When a man is diagnosed with terminal cancer, he takes custody of his misanthropic teenage son, for whom quality time means getting high, engaging in small-time prostitution, and avoiding his father. **My Two Cents:** This is one of my favorite movies, probably not on most lists, but for some odd reason I love it, so I thought I would include it.

☐ **Nashville (1975):** Over the course of a few hectic days, numerous interrelated people prepare for a political convention.

☐ **Once Upon a Time in America (1984):** A former Prohibition-era Jewish gangster returns to the Lower East Side of Manhattan over thirty years later, where he once again must confront the ghosts and regrets of his old life.

- ☐ **The Player (1992):** A Hollywood studio executive is being sent death threats by a writer whose script he rejected, but which one? **My Two Cents:** I met Tim Robbins and told him I just watched this movie recently and he asked if I saw his penis in it? Yep, that happened.

- ☐ **The Prestige (2006):** After a tragic accident, two stage magicians engage in a battle to create the ultimate illusion while sacrificing everything they have to outwit each other.

- ☐ **Raging Bull (1980):** The life of boxer Jake LaMotta, whose violence and temper that led him to the top in the ring destroyed his life outside of it. **Goof:** Joey and Jake attend a dance that occurs on "Saturday," 6 August 1941. This date was a Wednesday.

- ☐ **Rebel Without a Cause (1955):** A rebellious young man with a troubled past comes to a new town, finding friends and enemies.

- ☐ **The Shawshank Redemption (1994):** Two imprisoned men bond over a number of years, finding solace and eventual redemption through acts of common decency. **Fun Fact:** When Andy goes to the library to begin work as Brooks' assistant and Brooks' crow, Jake, is squawking, Tim Robbins had to time his line, "Hey, Jake. Where's Brooks?" so that the crow wouldn't squawk over him, since the bird could not be trained to squawk on cue. Robbins was able to adapt to this and time his line perfectly by learning the bird's squawking patterns, for which Writer and Director Frank Darabont praised him. Robbins' improvisation is noticeable, as he watches the bird carefully while approaching it, waiting for it to squawk, and doesn't begin his line until after it does so.

- ☐ **Sleuth (1972):** A man who loves games and theater invites his wife's lover to meet him, setting up a battle of wits with potentially deadly results.

- ☐ **Sunset Blvd (1950):** A screenwriter develops a dangerous relationship with a faded film star determined to make a triumphant return. **Misquote:** “I’m ready for my close-up, Mr. DeMille.”

Actual Quote: "*All right, Mr. DeMille.* I'm ready for my close-up."
Memorable Quote: *"I'm big. It's the pictures that got small."*

☐ **Sweet Smell of Success (1957):** Powerful but unethical Broadway columnist J.J. Hunsecker coerces unscrupulous press agent Sidney Falco into breaking up his sister's romance with a jazz musician. **Goof:** This acclaimed drama depicts the fraught relationship between a columnist and press agent, so one might expect it to portray newspapers with a relative degree of authenticity. On the contrary, the film repeats certain paragraphs over and over when Sidney Falco peruses J.J. Hunsecker's Broadway column.

☐ **There Will Be Blood (2007):** A story of family, religion, hatred, oil and madness, focusing on a turn-of-the-century prospector in the early days of the business.

☐ **Traffic (2000):** A conservative judge is appointed by the President to spearhead America's escalating war against drugs, only to discover that his teenage daughter is a crack addict. Two DEA agents protect an informant. A jailed drug baron's wife attempts to carry on the family business.

☐ **Trainspotting (1996):** Renton, deeply immersed in the Edinburgh drug scene, tries to clean up and get out, despite the allure of the drugs and influence of friends. **Memorable Quote:** We took morphine, diamorphine, cyclizine, codeine, temazepam, nitrazepam, phenobarbitone, sodium amytal, dextropropoxyphene, methadone, nalbuphine, pethidine, pentazocine, buprenorphine, dextromoramide, chlormethiazole. The streets are awash with drugs you can have for unhappiness and pain, and we took them all. Fuck it, we would have injected vitamin C if only they'd made it illegal.

☐ **The Truman Show (1998):** An insurance salesman discovers his whole life is actually a reality TV show.

☐ **Vertigo (1958):** A former police detective juggles wrestling with his personal demons and becoming obsessed with a hauntingly beautiful woman. **Goof:** Alfred Hitchcock's epic mystery-thriller is riddled with continuity issues—from Madeline losing a shoe in the water and having both on in the next scene, to a sailor walking by the flower shop twice in a row from the same direction. In another scene, as the camera pans away from Scottie as he stands at the tower's edge, the camera's shadow appears on the tower's exterior wall.

☐ **12 Angry Men (1957):** A jury holdout attempts to prevent a miscarriage of justice by forcing his colleagues to reconsider the evidence. **Goof:** There are 12 angry jurors in this heralded drama, and all but one think the defendant is guilty as charged. The lone holdout is Juror #8, who leaves the room to buy a knife and then introduces new evidence into the proceedings. In real life, these maneuvers would be grounds for a mistrial.

Family

This is your obvious feel-good movie that you may have watched as a kid or should watch with your children or nieces and nephews. For me, it's my nephews, as unfortunately, I can't have children. Or movies you want to watch alone and cherish the memories of being a kid.

- ☐ **Akeelah and the Bee (2006):** A young girl from South Los Angeles tries to make it to the National Spelling Bee.
- ☐ **Annie (1982):** A spunky young orphan is taken in by a rich eccentric, much to the chagrin of the cantankerous woman who runs the orphanage.
- ☐ **Babe (1995):** Babe, a pig raised by sheepdogs, learns to herd sheep with a little help from Farmer Hoggett. **My Favorite Line:** *"That'll do, pig. That'll do."*
- ☐ **Bedknobs and Broomsticks (1971):** An apprentice witch, three kids and a cynical magician conman search for the missing component to a magic spell to be used in the defense of Britain in World War II.
- ☐ **Beethoven (1992)**: A slobbering St. Bernard becomes the center of attention for a loving family, but must contend with a dog-napping veterinarian and his henchmen.
- ☐ **Bend it Like Beckham (2002):** Two ambitious girls, despite their parents' wishes, have their hearts set on careers in professional soccer. **Fun Fact:** Parminder Nagra was worried that the scar on her leg would prevent her from getting the role of Jess. Instead, the scar, and the story behind it, were worked into the script.

☐ **Big Daddy (1999):** A lazy law school grad adopts a kid to impress his girlfriend, but everything doesn't go as planned and he becomes the unlikely foster father.

☐ **The Black Stallion (1979):** A boy encounters a horse and bonds with him, later training him to race.

☐ **Bridge to Terabithia (1985):** When Leslie Burke moves in next door to Jess Aarons, Jess finds a friend in Leslie. Over time, they discover a secret place in the forest across a fallen pine tree, and over a creek, they call Terabithia, a place where memories are sacred. **Goof:** No bridge is ever seen or mentioned.

☐ **Charlotte's Web (1973):** Wilbur is a farm pig who's terrified that he'll end up on the dinner table. His friend Charlotte, a charming spider, comes to his rescue. She weaves words into her web, convincing the farmer that Wilbur is too special a pig to kill.

☐ **Cheaper By the Dozen (2003):** With his wife doing a book tour, a father of twelve must handle a new job and his unstable brood. **Fun Fact:** When the *Cheaper by the Dozen* movies were made, neither Steve Martin nor Bonnie Hunt, who played the parents of 12 children, had ever had a child in real life.

☐ **Chitty Chitty Bang Bang (1968):** A down-on-his-luck inventor turns a broken-down Grand Prix car into a fancy vehicle for his children, and then they go off on a magical fantasy adventure to save their grandfather in a far-off land.

☐ **Chronicles of Narnia (2005):** Four kids travel through a wardrobe to the land of Narnia and learn of their destiny to free it with the guidance of a mystical lion. **Fun Fact:** Georgie Henley's reaction to Mr. Tumnus at the lamppost is genuine. She had not seen her castmate James McAvoy in his costume before the scene was filmed, so her screams and reaction were real. Georgie's first reaction to the snowy world of Narnia is also genuine. She was carried into the set blindfolded to make her first entrance, and her wide-eyed, delighted reactions to it, all are entirely her own.

☐ **Dennis the Menace (1993):** When his parents have to go out of town, Dennis stays with Mr. and Mrs. Wilson. The little menace is driving Mr. Wilson crazy, but Dennis is just trying to be helpful. Even to the thief who's arrived in town.

☐ **Diary of a Wimpy Kid (2010):** The adventures of a 12-year-old who is fresh out of elementary and transitions to middle school, where he has to learn the consequences and responsibility to survive the year.

☐ **Doctor Dolittle (1998):** A doctor discovers that he can communicate with animals. **Fun Fact:** Eddie Murphy is terrified of live animals, and insisted that as many as possible be superimposed digitally in scenes. When he couldn't avoid acting in the same room as an animal, the shots frequently ended with Murphy screaming.

☐ **Enchanted (2007):** A young maiden in a land called Andalasia, who is prepared to be wed, is sent away to New York City by an evil Queen, where she falls in love with a lawyer.

☐ **Ever After (1998):** The Brothers Grimm arrive at the home of a wealthy Grande Dame who speaks of the many legends surrounding the fable of the cinder girl before telling the "true" story of her ancestor.

☐ **Free Willy (1993):** When a boy learns that a beloved killer whale is to be killed by the aquarium owners, the boy risks everything to free the whale. **My Two Cents:** After this movie I wanted to be a Zoologist, that quickly faded when I found out they make no money.

☐ **The Goonies (1985):** A group of young misfits called The Goonies discover an ancient map and set out on an adventure to find a legendary pirate's long-lost treasure.

☐ **Hachi: A Dog's Tale (2009):** A college professor bonds with an abandoned dog he takes into his home.

☐ **Home Alone (1990):** An eight-year-old troublemaker must protect his house from a pair of burglars when he is accidentally left home alone by his family during Christmas vacation. **Fun Fact:** Joe Pesci deliberately avoided Macaulay Culkin on-set, because he wanted Culkin to think he was mean. **My Two Cents:** I love the second one just as much as the first.

☐ **Homeward Bound (1993):** A fun-loving American bulldog pup, a hilarious Himalayan cat, and a wise old golden retriever embark on a long trek through the rugged wilderness of the Sierra Nevada mountains in a quest to reach home and their beloved owners.

☐ **Hook (1991):** When Captain James Hook kidnaps his children, an adult Peter Pan must return to Neverland and reclaim his youthful spirit in order to challenge his old enemy. **Goof:** Grandma Wendy tells Maggie that 80 years ago her neighbor enjoyed her stories of her and Peter so much that he began to write about them. The movie takes place in 1991. This would suggest that J.M. Barrie began writing about *Peter Pan* around 1911. However, the character Peter Pan first appeared in a book called, *The Little White Bird*, which was published in 1902, years prior to 1911. This makes Wendy's claim inaccurate.

☐ **Hugo (2001):** In 1931 Paris, an orphan living in the walls of a train station gets wrapped up in a mystery involving his late father and an automaton.

☐ **The Karate Kid (1984):** A martial arts master agrees to teach karate to a bullied teenager. **Memorable Quote:** *"Wax on, wax off."*

☐ **The Kid (1921):** The Tramp cares for an abandoned child, but events put that relationship in jeopardy.

☐ **The Kissing Booth (2018):** A high school student is forced to confront her secret crush at a kissing booth. **Fun Fact:** From June 2017 to autumn 2018, Joey King (Shelly 'Elle' Evans), and Jacob Elordi (Noah Flynn) were dating in real life.

☐ **Lemony Snicket's Series of Unfortunate Events (2004):** When a massive fire kills their parents, three children are delivered to the custody of cousin and stage actor Count Olaf, who is secretly plotting to steal their parents' vast fortune.

☐ **A Little Princess (1995):** A young girl is relegated to servitude at a boarding school when her father goes missing and is presumed dead. **Goof:** When Sara and Captain Crewe travel from India to the USA, a map is shown describing their route. The year is 1914 but the map is from the 1920s. Before WWI, Syria and Iraq didn't exist.

☐ **Little Rascals (1994):** Alfalfa is wooing Darla and his "He-Man-Woman-Hating" friends attempt to sabotage the relationship.

☐ **Maleficent (2014):** A vengeful fairy is driven to curse an infant princess, only to discover that the child may be the one person who can restore peace to their troubled land. **Fun Fact:** Angelina Jolie admitted that she scared little kids while in costume on the set of Maleficent, with one kid actually saying, "Mommy, please get the mean witch to stop talking to me." She adds that her daughter, Vivienne Jolie-Pitt, who played young Aurora, was the only child who was not scared of her.

☐ **Matilda (1996):** This film adaptation of a Roald Dahl work tells the story of Matilda Wormwood, a gifted girl forced to put up with a crude, distant father and mother.

☐ **Milo and Otis (1986):** The adventures of a young cat and a dog as they find themselves accidentally separated and each swept into a hazardous trek.

☐ **Mrs. Doubtfire (1993):** After a bitter divorce, an actor disguises himself as a female housekeeper to spend time with his children held in custody by his former wife. **Best Song:** "Dude Looks like a Lady"

- [ ] **My Girl (1991):** A young girl, on the threshold of her teen years, finds her life turning upside down, when she is accompanied by an unlikely friend.

- [ ] **The NeverEnding Story (1984):** A troubled boy dives into a wondrous fantasy world through the pages of a mysterious book. **Memorable Quote:** *"Never give up and good luck will find you."*

- [ ] **Pippy Longstocking (1969):** Pippi Longstocking, a super-strong redheaded little girl, moves into her father's house Villa Villekulla, and has adventures with her next-door neighbors Tommy and Annika in this compilation film of the classic European TV series.

- [ ] **The Princess Diaries (2001):** Mia Thermopolis has just found out that she is the heir apparent to the throne of Genovia. With her friends Lilly and Michael Moscovitz in tow, she tries to navigate through the rest of her sixteenth year.

- [ ] **Richie Rich (1994):** A rich young boy finds his family targeted in an inside job and must use his cunning to save them. **Fun Fact:** When the film was put into production, Macaulay Culkin was five foot two. A cast of tall adults were hired to create the illusion that Culkin was shorter than he actually was at the time. Most of the cast is taller than six feet.

- [ ] **School of Rock (2003):** After being kicked out of his rock band, Dewey Finn becomes a substitute teacher of an uptight elementary private school, only to try and turn his class into a rock band.

- [ ] **The Secret Garden (1993):** A young, recently-orphaned girl is sent to England after living in India all of her life. Once there, she begins to explore her new, seemingly-isolated surroundings, and its secrets. **Goof:** When Mary first meets Colin, as she enters his room, she is holding an oil lamp. The oil lamp, however, has a light bulb, not a wick and flame.

- [ ] **The Secret Life of Bees (2008):** In 1964, a teenage girl in search of the truth about her mother runs away to a small town in South

Carolina and finds a family of independent women who can connect her to her past.

☐ **Secondhand Lions (2003):** A coming-of-age story about a shy, young boy sent by his irresponsible mother to spend the summer with his wealthy, eccentric uncles in Texas.

☐ **The Sisterhood of the Travelling Pants (2005):** Four best girlfriends hatch a plan to stay connected with one another as their lives start off in different directions: they pass around a pair of secondhand jeans that fits each of their bodies perfectly. **Fun Fact:** Alexis Bledel went through a "summer camp" training to learn how to ride a Vespa and a mule, scuba dive, and took drawing lessons, in preparation for the movie.

☐ **Space Jam (1996):** In a desperate attempt to win a basketball match and earn their freedom, the Looney Tunes seek the aid of retired basketball champion, Michael Jordan.

☐ **Stand By Me (1986):** After the death of one of his friends, a writer recounts a childhood journey with his friends to find the body of a missing boy.

☐ **Uncle Buck (1989):** Bachelor and all-round slob Buck babysits his brother's rebellious teenage daughter and her cute younger brother and sister. **Memorable Quote:** *"Buck Melanoma. Moley Russell's wart. Not her wart. Not her wart! I'm... I'm the wart. She's my tumor. My... my growth. My... uh, my pimple. I'm Uncle Wart. Just old Buck "Wart" Russell. That's what they call me, or Melanoma Head. They'll call me that. "Melanoma Head's coming." I'm s... uncle! Maisy Russell's uncle!"* **Best Song:** "Wild Thing"

☐ **Willow (1988):** A young farmer is chosen to undertake a perilous journey in order to protect a special baby from an evil queen.

☐ **Willy Wonka and the Chocolate Factory (1971):** A poor but hopeful boy seeks one of the five coveted golden tickets that will send him on a tour of Willy Wonka's mysterious chocolate factory. **Fun Fact:** The Wonkatania was on a track in the chocolate river, but the actor playing the Oompa Loompa at the helm thought he was actually steering it. For the sake of believability, director Mel Stuart didn't tell him the truth.

☐ **The Witches (1990):** A young boy stumbles onto a witch convention and must stop them, even after he has been turned into a mouse.

Female Domination

This list includes all the badass women, all the women who won Academy Awards for Best Female in a Leading Role, all-around great performances, and maybe a few of my personal favorites, obvi. This list is longer than most as obviously this is a girl's guide to movies. These movies are about female empowerment and celebrating us. We are all amazing and we should all feel a sense of self-worth. Cheers to be awesome females!

- ☐ **The Accused (1988):** After a young woman suffers a brutal gang rape in a bar one night, a prosecutor assists in bringing the perpetrators to justice, including the ones who encouraged and cheered on the attack.

- ☐ **Alice Doesn't Live Here Anymore (1974):** A recently widowed woman is on the road with her precocious young son, determined to make a new life for herself as a singer. **Goof:** Tommy says the A7 chord hurts his fingers. A7 is one of the easiest chords, even for beginners. Kristofferson would know this and could have asked the script be altered, and recommend a more difficult chord.

- ☐ **Anastasia (1956):** An opportunistic businessman tries to pass off a mysterious impostor as the Grand Duchess Anastasia, and she is so convincing that even the biggest skeptics believe her.

- ☐ **Baby Face (1933):** A young woman, sexually exploited all her life, decides to turn the tables and exploit the hapless men at a big city bank - by gleefully seducing her way to the top.

- ☐ **Black Swan (2010):** A committed dancer struggles to maintain her sanity after winning the lead role in a production of Tchaikovsky's "Swan Lake." **Fun Fact:** Natalie Portman not only trained for a year as a dancer to prepare for the role, but paid for the training out of her own pocket until the film found investors. Aronofsky attributed the film's getting made at all to Portman's dedication and enthusiasm.

- ☐ **Blue Jasmine (2013):** A New York socialite, deeply troubled and in denial, arrives in San Francisco to impose upon her sister. She looks a million, but isn't bringing money, peace, or love...

- ☐ **Blue Sky (1994):** Jessica Lange stars in a period drama about a family moving to a military base, and she quickly becomes part of a cover-up involving nuclear bomb tests. **Fun Fact:** The film was completed in 1991, but was shelved and not released theatrically until three years later. This was due to studio production house Orion Pictures' bankruptcy.

- ☐ **Boys Don't Cry (1999):** A young man named Brandon Teena navigates love, life, and being transgender in rural Nebraska.

- ☐ **Bridget Jones' Diary (2001):** Bridget Jones is determined to improve herself while she looks for love in a year in which she keeps a personal diary. **Fun Fact:** To prepare for the role, Renée Zellweger gained 25 pounds, and then actually worked at a British publishing company for a month in preparation for the role. She adopted an alias as well as her posh accent and was apparently not recognized. On her desk in this office, she kept a framed picture of then boyfriend Jim Carrey. Workers who did not recognize her found this to be odd, but never mentioned it to her for fear of embarrassing her.

- ☐ **Buffy the Vampire Slayer (1992):** Flighty teenage girl Buffy Summers learns that she is her generation's destined battler of vampires.

- ☐ **Butterfield 8 (1960):** A beautiful New York model and socialite enjoys a very active night-life, but all things change when she falls for a married man and the consequences are tragic. **Fun Fact:** Dame Elizabeth Taylor and her husband, Mike Todd, had planned for *Cat on a Hot Tin Roof* (1958) to be her final movie, as she intended to retire from the screen. Todd had made a verbal agreement about this with MGM, but after his death, MGM forced Taylor to make this movie in order to fulfill the terms of her studio contract. As a result, Taylor refused to speak to director Daniel Mann for the entire production and hated this movie.

☐ **Caged (1950):** A naive 19-year-old widow becomes coarsened and cynical when she is sent to a women's prison and is exposed to hardened criminals and sadistic guards.

☐ **Charlie's Angels (2000):** Three women, detectives with a mysterious boss, retrieve stolen voice-ID software, using martial arts, tech skills, and sex appeal. **Goof:** It would be physically impossible to open an exit door on a pressurized aircraft during flight unless the cabin was first depressurized. But I guess that is the beauty of movies, right?

☐ **Children of a Lesser God (1986):** A new speech teacher at a school for the deaf falls in love with the janitor, a deaf woman speechless by choice.

☐ **Come Back, Little Sheba (1952):** An emotionally remote recovering alcoholic and his dowdy, unambitious wife face a personal crisis when they take in an attractive lodger.

☐ **Coquette (1929):** A flirtatious Southern belle is compromised with one of her suitors. **Memorable Quote:** *"Why, Michael, you look almost like you were dead!"*

☐ **Dangerous (1935):** An alcoholic actress who is considered a dangerous jinx is rehabilitated, but she then shows that she's as dangerous as ever.

☐ **The Devil Wears Prada (2011):** A graduate lands a job as an assistant to a demanding editor-in-chief of a fashion magazine. **Fun Fact:** On the first day of filming, Meryl Streep told Anne Hathaway, "I think you're perfect for the role. I'm so happy we're going to be working together." Then she paused and followed it up with, "That's the last nice thing I'll say to you." And it was. **Fun**

Fact: Many fashion designers allowed their clothes and accessories to be used in the film, making it the most expensively-costumed film in history. Meryl Streep donated her wardrobe to a charity auction. **Memorable Quote:** *"I'm just one stomach flu away from my goal weight."*

☐ **The Divorcee (1930):** When a woman discovers that her husband has been unfaithful to her, she decides to respond to his infidelities in kind.

☐ **Eat Drink Man Woman (1994):** A senior chef lives with his three grown daughters; the middle one finds her future plans affected by unexpected events and the life changes of the other household members. **Fun Fact:** As of 2016, this is the only film made by director Ang Lee to be set in his native Taiwan.

☐ **Eat Pray Love (2010):** A married woman realizes how unhappy her marriage really is, and that her life needs to go in a different direction. After a painful divorce, she takes off on a round-the-world journey to "find herself".

☐ **Erin Brockovich (2000):** Based on a true story. An unemployed single mother becomes a legal assistant and almost single-handedly brings down a California power company accused of polluting a city's water supply. **Memorable Quote:** *"Yeah. Yeah, sexy, huh? How 'bout this for a number? Six. That's how old my other daughter is, eight is the age of my son, two is how many times I've been married - and divorced; sixteen is the number of dollars I have in my bank account. 850-3943. That's my phone number, and with all the numbers I gave you, I'm guessing zero is the number of times you're gonna call it."*

☐ **Fences (2016):** A working-class African-American father tries to raise his family in the 1950s, while coming to terms with the events of his life.

☐ **The Farewell (2019):** A Chinese family discovers their grandmother has only a short while left to live and decide to keep her in the dark, scheduling a wedding to gather before she dies.

☐ **The Farmer's Daughter (1947):** After leaving her family's farm to study nursing in the city, a young woman finds herself on an unexpected path towards politics. **Fun Fact:** Initially titling their film *Katie for Congress*, RKO sought the more suggestive title *The Farmer's Daughter*. However, they had to buy that title from Paramount Pictures, who owned The Farmer's Daughter (1940).

☐ **The Favourite (2018):** In early 18th-century England, the status quo at the court is upset when a new servant arrives and endears herself to a frail Queen Anne.

☐ **Foxy Brown (1974):** A voluptuous black vigilante takes a job as a high-class prostitute to get revenge on the mobsters who murdered her boyfriend. **Goof:** In the farmhouse, Foxy Brown siphons gasoline from a barrel outside a window into a container inside the room. The siphon couldn't work, however, because the container is at a higher elevation than the barrel.

☐ **Fried Green Tomatoes (1991):** A housewife who is unhappy with her life befriends an old lady in a nursing home and is enthralled by the tales she tells of people she used to know.

☐ **Girl, Interrupted (1999):** Based on writer Susanna Kaysen's account of her 18-month stay at a mental hospital in the late 1960s. **Memorable Quotes:** *"Razors pain you, rivers are damp / Acid stains you, drugs cause cramps / Gun aren't lawful, nooses give / Gas smells awful, you might as well live."* **My Favorite Line:** *"You know what I think? I think you want to poop, Daisy. And I think it's been days."*

☐ **The Girl on the Train (2016):** A divorcee becomes entangled in a missing persons investigation that promises to send shockwaves throughout her life.

☐ **The Girl with the Dragon Tattoo (2011):** Journalist Mikael Blomkvist is aided in his search for a woman who has been missing for forty years by Lisbeth Salander, a young computer hacker. **Fun**

Fact: The film was released on December 20, exactly where the novel begins in chapter one.

☐ **The Heiress (1949):** A young naive woman falls for a handsome young man who her emotionally abusive father suspects is a fortune hunter.

☐ **The Help (2011):** An aspiring author during the civil rights movement of the 1960s decides to write a book detailing the African American maids' point of view on the white families for which they work, and the hardships they go through on a daily basis. **Memorable Quote:** *"You is kind. You is smart. You is important."*

☐ **The Hours (2002):** The story of how the novel "Mrs. Dalloway" affects three generations of women, all of whom, in one way or another, have had to deal with suicide in their lives.

☐ **Howards End (1992):** A businessman thwarts his wife's bequest of an estate to another woman.

☐ **Hud (1963):** Honest and hard-working Texas rancher Homer Bannon has a conflict with his unscrupulous, selfish, arrogant and egotistical son Hud, who sank into alcoholism after accidentally killing his brother in a car crash. **Fun Fact:** Patricia Neal is only in the movie for 21 minutes and 51 seconds, making her performance both the shortest to win a Best Actress Oscar and the shortest to win in a leading category.

☐ **I'm No Angel (1933):** Circus performer Tira seeks a better life pursuing the company of wealthy New York men with improbable comic complications along the way.

☐ **I Want to Live! (1958):** A prostitute, sentenced to death for murder, pleads her innocence. **Goof:** In her murder trial Barbara's attorney puts her on the witness stand where under cross examination the prosecution asks her about her previous conviction for perjury. No attorney, not even the worst court appointed attorney, would put a defendant on the witness stand knowing they had a previous conviction for perjury.

☐ **The Iron Lady (2011):** An elderly Margaret Thatcher talks to the imagined presence of her recently deceased husband as she struggles to come to terms with his death while scenes from her past life, from girlhood to British prime minister, intervene.

☐ **Jackie Brown (1997):** A middle-aged woman finds herself in the middle of a huge conflict that will either make her a profit or cost her life.

☐ **Jezebel (1938):** In 1850s Louisiana, a free-spirited Southern belle loses her fiancé due to her stubborn vanity and pride, and vows to win him back. **Fun Fact:** Bette Davis allegedly took 45 takes to perfect the scene where she lifts her riding skirt with her crop.

☐ **Johnny Belinda (1948):** A kind doctor volunteers to tutor a deaf-mute woman, but scandal starts to swirl when his pupil is raped and falls pregnant.

☐ **The Joy Luck Club (1993):** The life histories of four East Asian women and their daughters reflect and guide each other.

☐ **Judy (2019):** Legendary performer Judy Garland arrives in London in the winter of 1968 to perform a series of sold-out concerts. **Memorable Quote:** *"I love you all. You won't forget me, will you? Promise you won't."*

☐ **Kill Bill Vol. 1 and Vol. 2 (2003):** After awakening from a four-year coma, a former assassin wreaks vengeance on the team of assassins who betrayed her.

☐ **Kitty Foyle (1940):** A hard-working, white-collar girl from a middle-class family meets and falls in love with a young socialite, but she soon clashes with his family.

☐ **Klute (1971):** A small-town detective searching for a missing man has only one lead: a connection with a New York prostitute. **Fun Fact:** When Jane Fonda asked her father for advice on what to say for her Oscar acceptance speech, he suggested: "There's a great deal to say, but I'm not going to say it tonight."

☐ **Lady Bird (2017):** In 2002, an artistically inclined seventeen-year-old girl comes of age in Sacramento, California.

☐ **Lady Vengeance (2005):** After being wrongfully imprisoned for thirteen years and having her child taken away from her, a woman seeks revenge through increasingly brutal means.

☐ **A League of Their Own (1992):** Two sisters join a female professional baseball league and struggle to help it succeed. **My Favorite Line:** *"There's no crying in baseball!"*

☐ **Legally Blonde (2001):** Elle Woods, a fashionable sorority queen is dumped by her boyfriend and decides to follow him to law school. While there, she figures out that there is more to her than just looks.

☐ **Little Women (1994):** The March sisters live and grow in post-Civil War America. **Goof:** The soldiers' uniforms in the various party scenes have both stripes on the sleeves and shoulder boards. In reality, stripes on the sleeves denote an enlisted man, and shoulder boards denote an officer. They are thus mutually exclusive and both would not have been worn by the same individual.

☐ **Mildred Pierce (1945):** A hard-working mother inches towards disaster as she divorces her husband and starts a successful restaurant business to support her spoiled daughter.

☐ **Mommie Dearest (1981):** The abusive and traumatic adoptive upbringing of Christina Crawford at the hands of her mother, screen queen Joan Crawford, is depicted. **My Favorite Line:** *"No wire hangers, ever!"*

☐ **Monster (2003):** Based on the life of Aileen Wuornos, a Daytona Beach prostitute who became a serial killer.

☐ **Monster's Ball (2001):** After a family tragedy, a racist prison guard re-examines his attitudes while falling in love with the African-American wife of the last prisoner he executed.

☐ **Mulholland Drive (2001):** After a car wreck on Mulholland Drive renders a woman amnesiac, she and a Hollywood-hopeful search for clues and answers in a twisting venture beyond dreams and reality. **Fun Fact:** David Lynch originally wrote the basic idea for the story in the early 1990s, as a spin-off of *Twin Peaks* (1990). The character arc of Betty in the movie was written for *Twin Peaks* (1990) supporting character Audrey Horne, who would have been the central figure of the proposed spin-off.

☐ **Mystic Pizza (1988):** Three teenage girls come of age while working at a pizza parlor in a Connecticut town.

☐ **Norma Rae (1979):** A young single mother and textile worker agrees to help unionize her mill despite the problems and dangers involved.

☐ **On Golden Pond (1981):** Norman is a curmudgeon with an estranged relationship with his daughter Chelsea. At Golden Pond, he and his wife nevertheless agree to care for Billy, the son of Chelsea's new boyfriend, and a most unexpected relationship blooms. **Memorable Quote:** *"Listen to me, mister. You're my knight in shining armor. Don't you forget it. You're going to get back on that horse, and I'm going to be right behind you, holding on tight, away we're gonna go, go, go!"*

☐ **Panic Room (2002):** A divorced woman and her diabetic daughter take refuge in their newly-purchased house's safe room, when three men break-in, searching for a missing fortune.

☐ **Philomena (2013):** A world-weary political journalist picks up the story of a woman's search for her son, who was taken away from her decades ago after she became pregnant and was forced to live in a convent.

☐ **The Piano (1993):** In the mid-19th century, a mute woman is sent to New Zealand along with her young daughter and prized piano for an arranged marriage to a wealthy landowner, but is soon lusted after by a local worker on the plantation. **Fun Fact:** Holly

Hunter learned to play the piano when she was nine years old and played most of the piano sequences herself.

☐ **The Prime of Miss Jean Brodie (1969):** An eccentric Scottish schoolteacher's extravagantly romantic ideas about life--and love--overly impress her young pupils and bring her into conflict with her school's conservative headmistress.

☐ **The Queen (2006):** After the death of Princess Diana, Queen Elizabeth II struggles with her reaction to a sequence of events nobody could have predicted. **Goof:** The first meeting between Blair and the Queen is fiction. A newly-elected PM is always fully briefed on protocol before meeting the Monarch.

☐ **The Reader (2008):** Post-WWII Germany: Nearly a decade after his affair with an older woman came to a mysterious end, law student Michael Berg re-encounters his former lover as she defends herself in a war-crime trial.

☐ **Romy and Michele's High School Reunion (1997):** Two dim-witted, inseparable friends hit the road for their ten-year high school reunion and concoct an elaborate lie about their lives in order to impress their classmates. **Fun Fact:** Lisa Kudrow made up the entire "special glue" formula on the spot.

☐ **Room (2015):** Held captive for seven years in an enclosed space, a woman and her young son finally gain their freedom, allowing the boy to experience the outside world for the first time.

☐ **Room at the Top (1959):** An ambitious young accountant plots to wed a wealthy factory owner's daughter, despite falling in love with a married older woman. **Goof:** The story takes place in 1947, but all the women's fashions and hairstyles are strictly in the contemporary 1958 mode, when the film went before the cameras.

☐ **The Rose Tattoo (1955):** A Sicilian seamstress who idolizes her husband must deal with several family crises upon his sudden death.

- ☐ **Salt (2010):** A CIA agent goes on the run after a defector accuses her of being a Russian spy.

- ☐ **Sex and the City: The Movie (2008):** A New York City writer on sex and love is finally getting married to her Mr. Big. But her three best girlfriends must console her after one of them inadvertently leads Mr. Big to jilt her. **Memorable Quote:** *"You men have no idea what we're dealing with down there. Teeth placement, and jaw stress, and suction, and gag reflex, and all the while bobbing up and down, moaning and trying to breathe through our noses. Easy? Honey, they don't call it a job for nothing."*

- ☐ **Silkwood (1983):** A worker at a plutonium processing plant is purposefully contaminated, psychologically tortured and possibly murdered to prevent her from exposing worker safety violations at the plant.

- ☐ **Silver Lining Playbook (2012):** After a stint in a mental institution, former teacher Pat Solitano moves back in with his parents and tries to reconcile with his ex-wife. Things get more challenging when Pat meets Tiffany, a mysterious girl with problems of her own.

- ☐ **The Song of Bernadette (1943):** A young girl claims to have seen a divine vision, which prompts both a religious phenomenon and extreme skepticism. **Fun Fact:** The Imperial Prosecutor Vital Dutour who investigates Bernadette's visions, is portrayed in the movie as an atheist and anti-religious persecutor. In real life, however, Dutour was a devout Catholic who thought that Bernadette Soubirous' visions were hallucinations.

- ☐ **Sophie's Choice (1982):** Sophie is the survivor of Nazi concentration camps, who has found a reason to live with Nathan, a sparkling if unsteady American Jew obsessed with the Holocaust.

- ☐ **Steel Magnolias (1989):** A young beautician, newly arrived in a small Louisiana town, finds work at the local salon where a small group of women share a close bond of friendship and welcome her into the fold. **Goof:** At the end, when Annelle is nine months pregnant, she has a perm. Women should not get perms while pregnant, and a "hair technician" such as herself should know this.

☐ **Still Alice (2014):** A linguistics professor and her family find their bonds tested when she is diagnosed with Alzheimer's Disease.

☐ **A Streetcar Named Desire (1951):** Disturbed Blanche DuBois moves in with her sister in New Orleans and is tormented by her brutish brother-in-law while her reality crumbles around her. **Goof:** Marlon Brando is widely considered one of the greatest film actors of all time, but that doesn't mean he was always the most prepared. During a poker scene in this 1951 drama, Brando's Stanley Kowalski can be seen mimicking Stella's lines with his lips as if trying to recall the script from memory. **My Favorite Line:** *"SSSSTTTEEELLLLLAAA!!!!"* **Memorable Quote:** *"I have always depended on the kindness of strangers."*

☐ **Suffragette (2015):** In 1912 London, a young working mother is galvanized into radical political activism supporting the right for women to vote, and is willing to meet violence with violence to achieve this end.

☐ **Sunrise (1927):** A sophisticated urban woman seduces a farmer in the hopes that he will murder his neglected wife and join her in the city, but he soon finds himself rekindling his romance with the latter when she discovers their scheme.

☐ **Suspicion (1941):** A shy young heiress marries a charming gentleman, and soon begins to suspect he is planning to murder her. **Fun Fact:** Joan Fontaine won a Best Actress Oscar for this movie. Many pundits think she won because she did not win the previous year when she was nominated for *Rebecca* (1940).

☐ **Three Billboards Outside of Ebbing, Missouri (2017):** A mother personally challenges the local authorities to solve her daughter's murder when they fail to catch the culprit.

☐ **The Three Faces of Eve (1957):** A doctor treats a woman suffering from Multiple Personality Disorder.

☐ **The Trip to the Bountiful (1985):** In 1940s Texas, an elderly woman is determined to visit her childhood home for one last time. **Fun Fact:** Upon presenting the Best Actress Oscar to Geraldine Page in 1986, presenter F. Murray Abraham declared, "I consider this woman to be the greatest actress in the English language."

☐ **To Each His Own (1946):** An unwed mother, forced to give up her child to avoid scandal, follows her son's life from afar even as she prospers in business.

☐ **Touch of Class (1973):** Romantic comedy about a pair of clandestine lovers in a London-Spain tryst.

☐ **An Unmarried Woman (1978):** A wealthy woman from Manhattan's Upper East Side struggles to deal with her new identity and her sexuality after her husband of sixteen years leaves her for a younger woman. **Fun Fact:** Jill Clayburgh appears in every scene in the movie.

☐ **V for Vendetta (2005):** In a future British tyranny, a shadowy freedom fighter, known only by the alias of "V", plots to overthrow it with the help of a young woman.

☐ **White Oleander (2002):** A teenager journeys through a series of foster homes after her mother goes to prison for committing a crime of passion. **My Two Cents:** Although, again, probably not on many top movie lists, this is one of my favorite movies and amazing books.

☐ **Who's Afraid of Virginia Woolf? (1966):** A bitter, aging couple, with the help of alcohol, use their young houseguests to fuel anguish and emotional pain towards each other over the course of a distressing night.

☐ **Widows (2018):** Four women with nothing in common except a debt left behind by their dead husbands' criminal activities take fate into their own hands and conspire to forge a future on their own terms.

☐ **Winter's Bone (2010):** An unflinching Ozark Mountain girl hacks through dangerous social terrain as she hunts down her drug-dealing father while trying to keep her family intact. **Goof:** When Ree is in the boat about to use the chainsaw, there is no chain on the bar of the saw.

☐ **The Women (1939):** A study of the lives and romantic entanglements of various interconnected women.

☐ **Women in Love (1969):** Two best friends fall in love with a pair of women, but the relationships soon go in very different directions. **Fun Fact:** Glenda Jackson was the first actress to win an Oscar for a role that included nude scenes.

☐ **Women on the Verge of a Breakdown (1988):** A television actress encounters a variety of eccentric characters after embarking on a journey to discover why her lover abruptly left her.

☐ **Wonder Woman (2017):** When a pilot crashes and tells of conflict in the outside world, Diana, an Amazonian warrior in training, leaves home to fight a war, discovering her full powers and true destiny. **Fun Fact:** Gal Gadot was a part of re-shoots for the movie (including stunts) while being five months pregnant. Her baby bump was visible, so the crew created a costume which had a green screen around her belly, which was later removed during post-production.

☐ **Working Girl (1988):** When a secretary's idea is stolen by her boss, she seizes an opportunity to steal it back by pretending she has her boss' job.

☐ **9 to 5 (1980):** Three female employees of a sexist, egotistical, lying, hypocritical bigot find a way to turn the tables on him. **Best Song:** "9 to 5"

☐ **13 Going on 30 (2004):** A girl makes a wish on her thirteenth birthday, and wakes up the next day as a thirty-year-old woman.

Foreign Language

This list is compiled by many other lists I have found online and then searching on IMDB to make sure they had good ratings. This is one of the harder ones as I have not seen most of these films and going off other recommendations. I have only seen a select few and one I included because the concept was so interesting to me even though it wasn't on any lists and that one is *Love Me if You Dare.*

- ☐ **All About My Mother (1999):** Young Esteban wants to become a writer and also to discover the identity of his second mother, a trans woman, carefully concealed by his mother Manuela.

- ☐ **Aguirre, The Wrath of God (1972):** In the 16th century, the ruthless and insane Don Lope de Aguirre leads a Spanish expedition in search of El Dorado.

- ☐ **Amélie (2001):** Amélie is an innocent and naive girl in Paris with her own sense of justice. She decides to help those around her and, along the way, discovers love. **Fun Facts:** Audrey Tautou doesn't know how to skip stones; the stone-skipping scenes were made with special effects.

- ☐ **Amour (2012):** Georges and Anne are an octogenarian couple. They are cultivated, retired music teachers. Their daughter, also a musician, lives in Britain with her family. One day, Anne has a stroke, and the couple's bond of love is severely tested.

- ☐ **Amores Perros (2000):** A horrific car accident connects three stories, each involving characters dealing with loss, regret, and life's harsh realities, all in the name of love.

☐ **Andhadhun (2018):** A series of mysterious events change the life of a blind pianist, who must now report a crime that he should technically know nothing of. **Fun Fact:** Doctor Swami refers to Tabu as Lady Macbeth in a scene. This is an in-joke as Tabu played the role of Lady Macbeth in the Indian retelling of *Macbeth*, *Maqbool* (2003).

☐ **Andrei Rublev (1966):** The life, times and afflictions of the fifteenth-century Russian iconographer St. Andrei Rublev.

☐ **Ashes and Diamonds (1958):** As WWII and the German occupation ends, the Polish resistance and the Russian forces turn on each other in an attempt to take over leadership in Communist Poland.

☐ **Audition (1999):** A widower takes an offer to screen girls at a special audition, arranged for him by a friend to find him a new wife. The one he fancies is not who she appears to be after all. **Memorable Quote:** *"Words create lies. Pain can be trusted."*

☐ **Au Hasard Balthazar (1966):** The story of a mistreated donkey and the people around him. A study on saintliness and a sister piece to Bresson's Mouchette.

☐ **Autumn Sonata (1978):** A married daughter who longs for her mother's love is visited by the latter, a successful concert pianist.

☐ **The Bandit (1996):** Baran the Bandit, released from prison after 35 years, searches for vengeance and his lover. **Fun Fact:** This movie is exclusively regarded as the savior and the turning point of the Turkish cinema which was desperately struggling against the foreign films since 1980 and having difficulty to attract the domestic audience.

☐ **The Battle of Algiers (1966):** In the 1950s, fear and violence escalate as the people of Algiers fight for independence from the French government.

☐ **Bella de Jour (1967):** A frigid young housewife decides to spend her midweek afternoons as a prostitute.

☐ **Bicycle Thieves (1948):** In post-war Italy, a working-class man's bicycle is stolen. He and his son set out to find it. **Memorable Quote:** *"Why should I kill myself worrying when I'll end up just as dead?"*

☐ **The Bitter Tears of Petra Van Kant (1972):** A successful fashion designer abandons a sado-masochistic relationship with her female assistant in favor of a love affair with a beautiful young woman.

☐ **Breathless (1960):** A small-time thief steals a car and impulsively murders a motorcycle policeman. Wanted by the authorities, he reunites with a hip American journalism student and attempts to persuade her to run away with him to Italy.

☐ **A Brighter Summer Day (1991):** Based on a true story, primarily on a conflict between two youth gangs, a 14-year-old boy's girlfriend conflicts with the head of one gang for an unclear reason, until finally the conflict comes to a violent climax. **Fun Fact:** Raised in the U.S., actor Lisa Yang, who plays Ming, spoke her Mandarin dialogue with such a heavy accent that the director had her lines redubbed by another actress.

☐ **Capernaum (2018):** While serving a five-year sentence for a violent crime, a 12-year-old boy sues his parents for neglect.

☐ **Children of Heaven (1997):** After a boy loses his sister's pair of shoes, he goes on a series of adventures in order to find them. When he can't, he tries a new way to "win" a new pair.

☐ **Cinema Paradiso (1988):** A filmmaker recalls his childhood when falling in love with the pictures at the cinema of his home village and forms a deep friendship with the cinema's projectionist. **Goof:** The 1954 calendar is wrong. All the days are out by one. The calendar shows that 1st April, 1954 is a Friday. In fact, it was a Thursday.

☐ **City of God (2002):** In the slums of Rio, two kids' paths diverge as one struggles to become a photographer and the other a kingpin.

☐ **Close-Up (1990):** The true story of Hossain Sabzian, a cinephile who impersonated the director Mohsen Makhmalbaf to convince a family they would star in his so-called new film.

☐ **Come and See (1985):** After finding an old rifle, a young boy joins the Soviet resistance movement against ruthless German forces and experiences the horrors of World War II. **Fun Fact:** The original name of the film was supposed to be *Kill Hitler.* The name had to be changed because it was deemed inappropriate at that time.

☐ **The Conformist (1970):** A weak-willed Italian man becomes a fascist flunky who goes abroad to arrange the assassination of his old teacher, now a political dissident.

☐ **Dangal (2016):** Former wrestler Mahavir Singh Phogat and his two wrestler daughters struggle towards glory at the Commonwealth Games in the face of societal oppression.

☐ **Das Boot (1981):** The claustrophobic world of a WWII German U-boat; boredom, filth and sheer terror. **Goof:** Captain and several crew members are taking wave splashes/spray in their faces while standing on the bridge. The Captain keeps using his binoculars. If binocular lenses are wet, they are completely useless for their intended purpose.

☐ **Day of Wrath (1943):** The young wife of an aging priest falls in love with his son amidst the horror of a merciless witch hunt in 17th century Denmark.

☐ **The Death of Mr. Lãzãrescu (2005):** Mr. Lãzãrescu, a dying old man, is shuttled from hospital to hospital by a loyal paramedic as doctors refuse to operate and no one can agree on a diagnosis. **Fun Fact:** The film was shot in 39 nights in real hospitals. It was edited in 38 days.

☐ **Decalogue (2011):** An unemployed man opens a Church to live from the tithes. A teenager sells her body to buy the things her mother cannot buy for her. A young girl, sexually abused by her father, cannot accept he has moved out. A bitter man finds a purpose for his empty life in his best friend's wife. An Eastern European immigrant pushes his wife to work in a strip club to pay his debts. Five interlocked stories offer a provocative vision of the Ten Commandments and how nowadays, many people have to break them in order to survive.

☐ **Demon Slayer, Mugen Train (2020):** After his family was brutally murdered and his sister turned into a demon, Tanjiro Kamado's journey as a demon slayer began. Tanjiro and his comrades embark on a new mission aboard the Mugen Train, on track to despair.

☐ **Diabolique (1955):** The wife and mistress of a loathed school principal plan to murder him with what they believe is the perfect alibi. **Fun Fact:** Despite losing out on the chance to make the film, Alfred Hitchcock was a big fan of *Diabolique* (1955). Indeed, some state that it bore an influence on the making of *Psycho* (1960).

☐ **The Divine Bell and for the Butterfly (2007):** The true story of Elle editor Jean-Dominique Bauby who suffers a stroke and has to live with an almost totally paralyzed body; only his left eye isn't paralyzed.

☐ **The Discreet Charm of Bourgeoisie (1972):** A surreal, virtually plotless series of dreams centered around six middle-class people and their consistently interrupted attempts to have a meal together.

☐ **Downfall (2004):** Traudl Junge, the final secretary for Adolf Hitler, tells of the Nazi dictator's final days in his Berlin bunker at the end of WWII. **Fun Fact:** Bruno Ganz studied Parkinson's disease patients in a Swiss hospital to prepare for his role as Adolf Hitler.

☐ **The Earrings of Madame De… (1953):** When an aristocratic woman known only as "Madame de…" sells a pair of earrings given to her by her husband in order to pay some debts, she sets off a chain reaction of financial and carnal consequences that can end only in despair.

☐ **Fanny and Alexander (1982):** Two young Swedish children experience the many comedies and tragedies of their family, the Ekdahls.

☐ **A Fantastic Woman (2017):** Marina, a transgender woman who works as a waitress and moonlights as a nightclub singer, is bowled over by the death of her older boyfriend. **Memorable Quote:** *"Love isn't something you search for."*

☐ **Farewell My Concubine (1993):** Two boys meet at an opera training school in Peking in 1924. Their resulting friendship will span nearly 70 years and will endure some of the most troublesome times in China's history.

☐ **Flowers of Shanghai (1998):** In the "flower houses" (upscale brothels) of Shanghai, various interweaving stories of love, loyalty, and deceit play out subtly.

☐ **Gangs of Wasseypur (2012):** A clash between Sultan and Shahid Khan leads to the expulsion of Khan from Wasseypur, and ignites a deadly blood feud spanning three generations. **Fun Fact:** This is Bollywood's first commercial film to feature at the Cannes Film Festival during the Director's Fortnight segment at the festival (2012).

☐ **Grand Illusion (1937):** During WWI, two French soldiers are captured and imprisoned in a German P.O.W. camp. Several escape attempts follow until they are eventually sent to a seemingly inescapable fortress.

☐ **The Handmaiden (2016):** A woman is hired as a handmaiden to a Japanese heiress, but secretly she is involved in a plot to defraud her.

☐ **Hara-Kiri (1962):** When a ronin requesting seppuku at a feudal lord's palace is told of the brutal suicide of another ronin who previously visited, he reveals how their pasts are intertwined - and in doing so challenges the clan's integrity. **Memorable Quote:** *"What befalls others today, may be your own fate tomorrow."*

☐ **Heartbreaker (2010):** Alex and his sister run a business designed to break up relationships. They are hired by a rich man to break up the wedding of his daughter. The only problem is that they only have one week to do so.

☐ **High and Low (1963):** An executive of a shoe company becomes a victim of extortion when his chauffeur's son is kidnapped and held for ransom.

☐ **Hiroshima Mon Amour (1959):** A French actress filming an anti-war film in Hiroshima has an affair with a married Japanese architect as they share their differing perspectives on war. **Fun Fact:** This film pioneered the use of jump cutting to and from a flashback, and of very brief flashbacks to suggest obtrusive memories.

☐ **Howl's Moving Castle (2004):** When an unconfident young woman is cursed with an old body by a spiteful witch, her only chance of breaking the spell lies with a self-indulgent yet insecure young wizard and his companions in his legged, walking castle.

☐ **The Hunt (2012):** A teacher lives a lonely life, all the while struggling over his son's custody. His life slowly gets better as he finds love and receives good news from his son, but his new luck is about to be brutally shattered by an innocent little lie.

☐ **Ikiru (1952):** A bureaucrat tries to find a meaning in his life after he discovers he has terminal cancer. **Memorable Quote:** *"I can't afford to hate people. I don't have that kind of time."*

☐ **Incendies (2010):** Twins journey to the Middle East to discover their family history and fulfill their mother's last wishes.

☐ **In the Mood for Love (2000):** Two neighbors form a strong bond after both suspect extramarital activities of their spouses. However, they agree to keep their bond platonic so as not to commit similar wrongs.

- ☐ **The Intouchables (2011):** After he becomes a quadriplegic from a paragliding accident, an aristocrat hires a young man from the projects to be his caregiver. **Goof:** Driving north to Dunkirk at the end would have taken place in the morning after their night adventure. The sun would have been rising in the east, instead of setting in the west. So, either the time of day is wrong, or the direction they are driving.

- ☐ **Jeanne Dielman, 23 Commerce Quay, 1080 Brussels (1975):** A lonely widowed housewife does her daily chores, takes care of her apartment where she lives with her teenage son, and turns the occasional trick to make ends meet. However, something happens that changes her safe routine.

- ☐ **Jodhaa Akbar (2008):** A sixteenth century love story about a marriage of alliance that gave birth to true love between a great Mughal emperor, Akbar, and a Rajput princess, Jodha.

- ☐ **The Killer (1989):** A disillusioned assassin accepts one last hit in hopes of using his earnings to restore vision to a singer he accidentally blinded. **Fun Fact:** John Woo dedicated this film to Martin Scorsese.

- ☐ **La Vie en Rose (2007):** Biopic of the iconic French singer Édith Piaf. Raised by her grandmother in a brothel, she was discovered while singing on a street corner at the age of 19. Despite her success, Piaf's life was filled with tragedy.

- ☐ **L'Avventura (1960):** A woman disappears during a Mediterranean boating trip. During the search, her lover and her best friend become attracted to each other.

- ☐ **La Dolce Vita (1960):** A series of stories following a week in the life of a philandering tabloid journalist living in Rome. **Memorable Quote:** *"A man who agrees to live like this is a finished man, he's nothing but a worm! I don't believe in your aggressive, sticky,* *maternal love! I don't want it; I have no use for it! This isn't love, it's brutalization!"*

- ☐ **La Haine (1995):** 24 hours in the lives of three young men in the French suburbs the day after a violent riot.

- ☐ **Léon: The Professional (1994):** Mathilda, a 12-year-old girl, is reluctantly taken in by Léon, a professional assassin, after her family is murdered. An unusual relationship forms as she becomes his protégée and learns the assassin's trade. Based on the book *Silas Marner* by George Eliot.

- ☐ **The Leopard (1963):** The Prince of Salina, a noble aristocrat of impeccable integrity, tries to preserve his family and class amid the tumultuous social upheavals of 1860's Sicily. **Goof:** *The Leopard* makes several historical blunders. One notable mistake comes early in the movie, when the Prince uses the word "mafiosi," which didn't enter the common lexicon until several years after the movie is set, thanks to the opera *I Mafiusi de la Vicaria.*

- ☐ **Life is Beautiful (1997):** When an open-minded Jewish librarian and his son become victims of the Holocaust, he uses a perfect mixture of will, humor, and imagination to protect his son from the dangers around their camp.

- ☐ **Like Stars on Earth (2007):** An eight-year-old boy is thought to be a lazy trouble-maker, until the new art teacher has the patience and compassion to discover the real problem behind his struggles in school.

- ☐ **The Lives of Others (2006):** In 1984 East Berlin, an agent of the secret police, conducting surveillance on a writer and his lover, finds himself becoming increasingly absorbed by their lives. **Fun Fact:** All the listening/recording props in the film are actual Stasi equipment on loan from museums and collectors. The props master had spent two years in a Stasi prison, and insisted upon absolute authenticity, down to the machine used to steam-open up to 600 letters per hour.

☐ **Love Me if You Dare (2003):** As adults, best friends Julien and Sophie continue the odd game they started as children -- a fearless competition to outdo one another with daring and outrageous stunts. While they often act out to relieve one another's pain, their game might be a way to avoid the fact that they are truly meant for one another. **My Two Cents:** This is another one of my picks. It's so different in its story telling and why I think it is a must watch. I know, I know I stated this in the intro, but it's ok to state again.

☐ **M (1931):** When the police in a German city are unable to catch a child-murderer, other criminals join in the manhunt.

☐ **Memories of Murder (2003):** In a small Korean province in 1986, two detectives struggle with the case of multiple young women being found raped and murdered by an unknown culprit.

☐ **Metropolis (1927):** In a futuristic city sharply divided between the working class and the city planners, the son of the city's mastermind falls in love with a working-class prophet who predicts the coming of a savior to mediate their differences. **Goof:** A pioneering movie in the science-fiction genre, the silent film *Metropolis* was one of the first full-length features to be set in a distant future. Although its events took place millennia after the 1920s, the creative team wasn't very imaginative when it came to illustrating what that future may look like. Characters in the movie still dress in top hats and coattails, phones are still clunky and corded, and cars haven't evolved at all beyond Model A's and Studebaker Dictators.

☐ **Mishima (1985):** A fictionalized account in four chapters of the life of celebrated Japanese writer Yukio Mishima.

☐ **Murder in Cell No. 7 (2019):** A story of love between a mentally-ill father who was wrongly accused of murder and his lovely six-year-old daughter. Prison will be their home. Based on the 2013 Korean movie *7-beon-bang-ui seon-mul* (2013).

☐ **My Father and My Son (2005):** The family of a left-wing journalist is torn apart after the military coup of Turkey in 1980.

Memorable Quotes: *"As people grow, do their dreams get smaller, dad?"*

☐ **My Neighbor Tutoro (1988):** When two girls move to the country to be near their ailing mother, they have adventures with the wondrous forest spirits who live nearby.

☐ **My Night at Maud's (1969):** The rigid principles of a devout Catholic man are challenged during a one-night stay with Maud, a divorced woman with an outsize personality.

☐ **Nausicaa of the Valley of the Wind (1984):** Warrior and pacifist Princess Nausicaä desperately struggles to prevent two warring nations from destroying themselves and their dying planet. **Goof:** During the invasion, one of the large carrier planes is seen moving backwards.

☐ **Nosferatu, A Symphony of Terror (1922):** Vampire Count Orlok expresses interest in a new residence and real estate agent Hutter's wife.

☐ **Oldboy (2003):** After being kidnapped and imprisoned for fifteen years, Oh Dae-Su is released, only to find that he must find his captor in five days.

☐ **Pan's Labyrinth (2006):** In the Falangist Spain of 1944, the bookish young stepdaughter of a sadistic army officer escapes into an eerie but captivating fantasy world. **Fun Fact:** Guillermo del Toro repeatedly refused offers from Hollywood producers, in spite of being offered double the budget provided the film was made in English. He didn't want any compromise in the storyline to suit the "market needs."

☐ **Pather Panchali (1955):** Impoverished priest Harihar Ray, dreaming of a better life for himself and his family, leaves his rural Bengal village in search of work.

☐ **Persona (1966):** A nurse is put in charge of a mute actress and finds that their personae are melding together.

☐ **Playtime (1967):** Monsieur Hulot curiously wanders around a high-tech Paris, paralleling a trip with a group of American tourists. Meanwhile, a nightclub/restaurant prepares its opening night, but it's still under construction. **Fun Fact:** The film's failure at the box office kept Jacques Tati in debt for several years.

☐ **Princess Mononoke (1997):** On a journey to find the cure for a Tatarigami's curse, Ashitaka finds himself in the middle of a war between the forest gods and Tatara, a mining colony. In this quest he also meets San, the Mononoke Hime.

☐ **Raatchasan (2018):** A sub-inspector sets out in pursuit of a mysterious serial killer who targets teen school girls and murders them brutally.

☐ **Raise the Red Lantern (1991):** A young woman becomes the fourth wife of a wealthy lord, and must learn to live with the strict rules and tensions within the household. **Fun Fact:** This film was banned in China for a short time in the early 1990s.

☐ **Ran (1985):** In Medieval Japan, an elderly warlord retires, handing over his empire to his three sons. However, he vastly underestimates how the new-found power will corrupt them and cause them to turn on each other...and him.

☐ **Rashomon (1950):** The rape of a bride and the murder of her samurai husband are recalled from the perspectives of a bandit, the bride, the samurai's ghost and a woodcutter.

☐ **Rififi (1955):** Four men plan a technically perfect crime, but the human element intervenes... **Goof:** While the jewelry store robbery goes off without a hitch, that wasn't the case for the on-screen rehearsal. In the scene where Tony and Mario time the escape drive, the license plate on their getaway car changes from 2126-DB75 to 3510-BU75.

☐ **Ringu (1998):** A reporter and her ex-husband investigate a cursed video tape that is rumored to kill the viewer seven days after watching it.

☐ **The Rules of the Game (1939):** A bourgeois life in France at the onset of World War II, as the rich and their poor servants meet up at a French chateau.

☐ **Run Lola Run (1998):** After a botched money delivery, Lola has 20 minutes to come up with 100,000 Deutschmarks. **My Two Cents:** How I learned the word shit in German.

☐ **Sansho the Bailiff (1954):** In medieval Japan, a compassionate governor is sent into exile. His wife and children try to join him, but are separated, and the children grow up amid suffering and oppression.

☐ **The Secret in Their Eyes (2009):** A retired legal counselor writes a novel hoping to find closure for one of his past unresolved homicide cases and for his unreciprocated love with his superior - both of which still haunt him decades later.

☐ **A Separation (2011):** A married couple are faced with a difficult decision - to improve the life of their child by moving to another country or to stay in Iran and look after a deteriorating parent who has Alzheimer's disease. **Fun Fact:** First Iranian film to win an Oscar.

☐ **Séraphine (2008):** Based on the life of French painter Séraphine de Senlis.

☐ **Seven Samurai (1954):** A poor village under attack by bandits recruits seven unemployed samurai to help them defend themselves. **Goof:** One of the most influential films in cinematic history, "Seven Samurai" is about a village of farmers who hire seven masterless samurai to protect them from the bandits who attempt to steal their crops each year. Groundbreaking though it may be, the film still contains several anachronistic errors, like the two back-to-back musket shots in the final battle that come from a single musket. At the time, muskets couldn't be reloaded that quickly, meaning such rapid fire would have been impossible.

☐ **The Seventh Seal (1957):** A man seeks answers about life, death, and the existence of God as he plays chess against the Grim Reaper during the Black Plague.

☐ **Shoah (1985):** Claude Lanzmann's epic documentary recounts the story of the Holocaust through interviews with witnesses - perpetrators as well as survivors.

☐ **A Silent Voice (2016):** A young man is ostracized by his classmates after he bullies a deaf girl to the point where she moves away. Years later, he sets off on a path for redemption. **Fun Fact:** Shoko's English dub voice actress Lexi Marman is actually deaf in real life.

☐ **The Spirit of the Beehive (1973):** In 1940, after watching and being traumatized by the movie *Frankenstein* (1931), a sensitive seven-year-old girl living in a small Spanish village drifts into her own fantasy world.

☐ **Solaris (1972):** A psychologist is sent to a station orbiting a distant planet in order to discover what has caused the crew to go insane.

☐ **Stalker (1979):** A guide leads two men through an area known as the Zone to find a room that grants wishes. **Memorable Quote:** *"A man writes because he is tormented, because he doubts. He needs to constantly prove to himself and the others that he's worth something. And if I know for sure that I'm a genius? Why write then? What the hell for?"*

☐ **Three Colors, Red (1994):** A model discovers a retired judge is keen on invading people's privacy.

☐ **Tokyo Story (1953):** An old couple visit their children and grandchildren in the city, but receive little attention.

☐ **The Umbrellas of Cherbourg (1964):** A young woman separated from her lover by war faces a life-altering decision. **Fun Fact:** The umbrella shop still exists at 13 Rue De Port, Cherbourg and is marked with a plaque commemorating the film.

- ☐ **Viridiana (1961):** Viridiana, a young nun about to take her final vows, pays a visit to her widowed uncle at the request of her Mother Superior.

- ☐ **The Wages of Fear (1953):** In a decrepit South American village, four men are hired to transport an urgent nitroglycerine shipment without the equipment that would make it safe.

- ☐ **When a Woman Ascends the Stairs (1960):** A middle-aged bar hostess, constantly in debt, is faced with numerous social constraints and challenges posed to her by her family, customers and friends. **Memorable Quote:** *"Bars in the daytime are like women without makeup.:*

- ☐ **Wild Strawberries (1957):** After living a life marked by coldness, an aging professor is forced to confront the emptiness of his existence.

- ☐ **Wild Tales (2014):** Six short stories that explore the extremities of human behavior involving people in distress.

- ☐ **Wings of Desire (1987):** An angel tires of overseeing human activity and wishes to become human when he falls in love with a mortal. **Goof:** Upon waking Damiel is hit by a cuirass presumably thrown from the helicopter he sees above. If a 10-pound piece of armor was dropped by a helicopter at 100 feet it would exert over 635 pounds of force on Damiel, more than the 520 necessary to crush his skull. Even if it doesn't hit him directly it would hurt him much more than it appears to.

- ☐ **Yi Yi (One and a Two) (2000):** Each member of a middle-class Taipei family seeks to reconcile past and present relationships within their daily lives.

- ☐ **Yojimbo (1961):** A crafty ronin comes to a town divided by two criminal gangs and decides to play them against each other to free the town.

☐ **Your Name (2016):** Two strangers find themselves linked in a bizarre way. When a connection forms, will distance be the only thing to keep them apart? **Memorable Quote:** *"Treasure the experience. Dreams fade away after you wake up."*

☐ **3 Idiots (2009):** Two friends are searching for their long-lost companion. They revisit their college days and recall the memories of their friend who inspired them to think differently, even as the rest of the world called them "idiots".

☐ **8 ½ (1963):** A harried movie director retreats into his memories and fantasies. **Fun Fact:** David Lynch's favorite movie.

☐ **The 400 Blows (1959):** A young boy, left without attention, delves into a life of petty crime.

Holiday

We all know the great classics that we watch during the Holiday season such as Halloween and Christmas or whatever you choose to celebrate. I, myself, always tune into a great love story on Lifetime or whatever their 24 days of Christmas is. I do what most normal females do, look on IMDB and see how hot the guy is in the film. If I find him a little attractive, I will definitely watch, regardless of the premise. Am I the only one who does this? No? Ok good, thanks for making me feel better about my decisions.

- ☐ **The Addams Family (1991):** Con artists plan to fleece an eccentric family using an accomplice who claims to be their long-lost uncle. **Best Song:** "The Addams Groove"

- ☐ **Bad Santa (2003):** A miserable conman and his partner pose as Santa and his Little Helper to rob department stores on Christmas Eve. But they run into problems when the conman befriends a troubled kid.

- ☐ **Beetlejuice (1988):** The spirits of a deceased couple are harassed by an unbearable family that has moved into their home, and hire a malicious spirit to drive them out.

- ☐ **The Bishop's Wife (1947):** A debonair angel comes to Earth to help an Episcopalian bishop and his wife in their quest to raise money for the new church. **My Two Cents:** Of course, you can also watch the remake with the late, great Whitney Houston in *The Preacher's Wife.*

- ☐ **Casper (1995):** An afterlife therapist and his daughter meet a friendly young ghost when they move into a crumbling mansion in order to rid the premises of wicked spirits. **My Two Cents:** Obviously, Devon Sawa was my heartthrob in the 90s.

☐ **A Christmas Story (1983):** In the 1940s, a young boy named Ralphie attempts to convince his parents, his teacher and Santa that a Red Ryder BB gun really is the perfect Christmas gift.

☐ **Elf (2003):** Raised as an over-sized elf, a human travels from the North Pole to NYC to meet his biological father who doesn't know he exists and is in desperate need of some Christmas spirit. **Memorable Quote:** *"I thought maybe we could make ginger bread houses, and eat cookie dough, and go ice skating, and maybe even hold hands."*

☐ **The Family Stone (2005):** An uptight, conservative businesswoman accompanies her boyfriend to his eccentric and outgoing family's annual Christmas celebration and finds that she's a fish out of water in their free-spirited way of life. **Memorable Quote:** *"Brad? Brad Stevenson? Aren't you the guy who popped Amy's cherry?"*

☐ **Hocus Pocus (1993):** A curious youngster moves to Salem, where he struggles to fit in before awakening a trio of diabolical witches that were executed in the 17th century.

☐ **The Holiday (2006):** Two women troubled with guy-problems swap homes in each other's countries, where they each meet a local guy and fall in love.

☐ **How the Grinch Stole Christmas (1966):** A grumpy hermit hatches a plan to steal Christmas from the Whos of Whoville. **Fun Fact:** Thurl Ravenscroft, who sang the song, is best known as the voice of Tony the Tiger in numerous Frosted Flakes TV commercials. Thurl was picked to sing these songs because his voice was an extremely deep bass.

☐ **I'll be Home for Christmas (1998):** A college student faces an impossible journey when he is left stranded in the desert, thousands of miles from home, with no money and only a few days left until Christmas.

- ☐ **It's a Wonderful Life (1946):** An angel is sent from Heaven to help a desperately frustrated businessman by showing him what life would have been like if he had never existed. Free on NBC every Christmas. **Memorable Quote:** *"Every time a bell rings, an angel gets his wings."*

- ☐ **Jack Frost (1998):** A father who can't keep his promises dies in a car accident. One year later, he returns as a snowman who has the final chance to put things right with his son before he is gone forever.

- ☐ **Jingle All the Way (1996):** A father vows to get his son a Turbo Man action figure for Christmas. However, every store is sold out of them, and he must travel all over town and compete with everybody else in order to find one.

- ☐ **Last Holiday (2006):** Upon learning of a terminal illness, a shy woman decides to sell all her possessions and live it up at a posh Central European hotel. **Goof:** The croupier at the roulette table announces "no more bets" and then Kragen puts his bet on the table. At a real casino he would have been asked to remove his bet, since betting was closed.

- ☐ **Last Christmas (2019):** Kate is a young woman subscribed to bad decisions. Working as an elf in a year-round Christmas store is not good for the wannabe singer. However, she meets Tom there. Her life takes a new turn. For Kate, it seems too good to be true.

- ☐ **Love Actually (2003):** The film follows the lives of eight very different couples as they deal with their love lives in various loosely interrelated tales, all set during a frantic month before Christmas in London, England. **My Favorite Line:** *"To me, you are perfect."*

- ☐ **Miracle on 34th Street (1947):** When a nice old man who claims to be Santa Claus is institutionalized as insane, a young lawyer decides to defend him by arguing in court that he is the real thing. The remake with Mara Wilson is equally as cute.

☐ **National Lampoon's Christmas Vacation (1989):** The Griswold family's plans for a big family Christmas predictably turn into a big disaster. **My Favorite Line:** *"Why is the carpet all wet, *Todd*?" "I don't *know*, Margo!"* **Memorable Quote:** *"Merry Christmas. Shitter was full."*

☐ **New Year's Eve (2011):** The lives of several couples and singles in New York City intertwine over the course of New Year's Eve.

☐ **The Santa Clause (1994):** When a man inadvertently makes Santa fall off of his roof on Christmas Eve, he finds himself magically recruited to take his place.

☐ **Scrooged (1988):** A selfish, cynical television executive is haunted by three spirits bearing lessons on Christmas Eve. **Fun Fact:** Bill Murray turned down the lead roles in *Rain Man* (1988), *Big* (1988) and *Cocktail* (1988) to make this film.

☐ **The Witches of Eastwick (1987):** Three single women in a picturesque village have their wishes granted, at a cost, when a mysterious and flamboyant man arrives in their lives.

☐ **200 Cigarettes (1999):** A collection of twentysomethings try to cope with relationships, loneliness, desire and their individual neuroses.

Horror

A horror film is one that seeks to elicit fear or disgust in its audience for entertainment purposes. Horror films additionally aim to evoke viewers' nightmares, revulsions and terror of the unknown or the macabre. Initially inspired by literature from authors such as Edgar Allan Poe, Bram Stoker, and Mary Shelley, horror has existed as a film genre for more than a century. Horror may also overlap with the fantasy, supernatural fiction, and thriller genres.

Plots within the horror genre often involve the intrusion of an evil force event, or personage into the everyday world. Prevalent elements include ghosts, vampires, werewolves, evil witches, cults, black magic, demons and demonic possession, Satanism and the Devil, monsters, mummies, ETs, zombies, dystopian or apocalyptic worlds, disturbed children, gore and torture, cannibalism, natural forces, evil clowns, psychopaths and serial killers.

☐ **An American Werewolf in London (1981):** Two American college students on a walking tour of Britain are attacked by a werewolf that none of the locals will admit exists.

☐ **Angel Heart (1987):** A private investigator is hired by a man who calls himself Louis Cyphre to track down a singer named Johnny Favorite. But the investigation takes an unexpected and somber turn. **Fun Fact:** Writer and director Alan Parker claims that Robert De Niro's performance as Louis Cyphre was so eerie and realistic that he generally avoided him during his scenes, letting him just direct himself.

☐ **The Birds (1963):** A wealthy San Francisco socialite pursues a potential boyfriend to a small Northern California town that slowly takes a turn for the bizarre when birds of all kinds suddenly begin to attack people.

☐ **The Blair Witch Project (1999):** Three film students vanish after traveling into a Maryland forest to film a documentary on the local Blair Witch legend, leaving only their footage behind.

☐ **Bride of Frankenstein (1935):** Mary Shelley reveals the main characters of her novel survived: Dr. Frankenstein, goaded by an even madder scientist, builds his monster a mate. **Memorable Quote:** *"To a new world of gods and monsters!"*

☐ **Carrie (1976):** Carrie White, a shy, friendless teenage girl who is sheltered by her domineering, religious mother, unleashes her telekinetic powers after being humiliated by her classmates at her senior prom.

☐ **Child's Play (1988):** A single mother gives her son a much sought-after doll for his birthday, only to discover that it is possessed by the soul of a serial killer.

☐ **Dead of Night (1945):** Architect Walter Craig senses impending doom as his half-remembered recurring dream turns into reality. The guests at the country house encourage him to stay as they take turns telling supernatural tales. **Fun Fact:** The film's structure was influential in the way the "Amicus" horror films were made.

☐ **Deliverance (1972):** Intent on seeing the Cahulawassee River before it's dammed and turned into a lake, outdoor fanatic Lewis Medlock takes his friends on a canoeing trip they'll never forget into the dangerous American back-country.

☐ **Don't Look Now (1973):** A married couple grieving the recent death of their young daughter are in Venice when they encounter two elderly sisters, one of whom is psychic and brings a warning from beyond.

☐ **Dracula (1992):** The centuries old vampire Count Dracula comes to England to seduce his barrister Jonathan Harker's fiancée Mina Murray and inflict havoc in the foreign land. **Goof:** In the opening scene, it says that Constantinople was captured by the Turks in year 1462. In actuality, it was captured by the Turks on May 29, 1453.

☐ **Eraserhead (1977):** Henry Spencer tries to survive his industrial environment, his angry girlfriend, and the unbearable screams of his newly born mutant child.

☐ **The Evil Dead (1981):** Five friends travel to a cabin in the woods, where they unknowingly release flesh-possessing demons.

☐ **The Exorcist (1973):** When a 12-year-old girl is possessed by a mysterious entity, her mother seeks the help of two priests to save her. **Fun Fact:** The scene where Regan projectile vomits at Father Karras only required one take. The vomit was intended to hit Jason Miller in the chest, but the plastic tubing misfired, hitting him in the face. His reaction of shock and disgust while wiping away the vomit is genuine, and Miller admitted in an interview that he was very angered by this mistake.

☐ **Fatal Attraction (1987):** A married man's one-night stand comes back to haunt him.

☐ **The Fog (1980):** An unearthly fog rolls into a small coastal town exactly 100 years after a ship mysteriously sank in its waters.

☐ **Freaks (1932):** A circus' beautiful trapeze artist agrees to marry the leader of side-show performers, but his deformed friends discover she is only marrying him for his inheritance. **Memorable Quote:** *"You dirty, slimy, freaks! Freaks, freaks, freaks! You fools! Make me one of you, will you?"*

☐ **Friday the 13th (1980):** A group of camp counselors are stalked and murdered by an unknown assailant while trying to reopen a summer camp which was the site of a child's drowning and a grisly double murder years before.

☐ **Gremlins (1984):** A young man inadvertently breaks three important rules concerning his new pet and unleashes a horde of malevolently mischievous monsters on a small town.

☐ **Halloween (1978):** Fifteen years after murdering his sister on Halloween night 1963, Michael Myers escapes from a mental hospital and returns to the small town of Haddonfield, Illinois to kill again. **Fun Fact:** The Michael Myers face mask in Halloween is just a Captain Kirk/William Shatner face mask. They spray-painted the face white, teased out the hair, and reshaped the eye holes.

☐ **The Haunting (1963):** Hill House has stood for about 90 years and appears haunted: its inhabitants have always met strange, tragic ends. Now Dr. John Markway has assembled a team of people who he thinks will prove whether or not the house is haunted.

☐ **It (2017):** In the summer of 1989, a group of bullied kids band together to destroy a shape-shifting monster, which disguises itself as a clown and preys on the children of Derry, their small Maine town. **Fun Fact:** The Duffer Brothers originally wanted to direct the movie, but were overlooked as they were not "established" enough. They went on to create *Stranger Things* (2016), which co-stars Finn Wolfhard (Richie) and pays homage to Stephen King.

☐ **Jaws (1975):** When a killer shark unleashes chaos on a beach community, it's up to a local sheriff, a marine biologist, and an old seafarer to hunt the beast down. **Misquote:** "We're going to need a bigger boat." **Actual Quote:** "*You're* going to need a bigger boat." **Fun Fact:** That quote wasn't actually in the script and was improvised. **Fun Fact:** Author Peter Benchley plays the role of a TV reporter in *Jaws*. Benchley was reportedly thrown off set after continually arguing with Spielberg about the film's ending.

☐ **King Kong (1933):** A film crew goes to a tropical island for an exotic location shoot and discovers a colossal ape who takes a shine to their female blonde star. He is then captured and brought back to New York City for public exhibition. **Misquote:** "Twas beauty *that* killed the beast." **Actual Quote:** "It was Beauty killed the Beast."

☐ **The Lost Boys (1987):** After moving to a new town, two brothers discover that the area is a haven for vampires. **My Two Cents:** My mom's favorite horror movie.

☐ **Manhunter (1986):** Former FBI profiler Will Graham returns to service to pursue a deranged serial killer dubbed "the Tooth Fairy" by the media.

☐ **Misery (1990):** After an author is rescued by a fan, he realizes the care is only the beginning of a nightmare.

☐ **The Mummy (1999):** At an archaeological dig in the ancient city of Hamunaptra, an American serving in the French Foreign Legion accidentally awakens a mummy who begins to wreak havoc as he searches for the reincarnation of his long-lost love. **Fun Fact:** Brendan Fraser nearly died during a scene where his character is hanged. Rachel Weisz remembered, "He stopped breathing and had to be resuscitated."

☐ **A Nightmare on Elm Street (1984):** The monstrous spirit of a slain child murderer seeks revenge by invading the dreams of teenagers whose parents were responsible for his untimely death.

☐ **Night of the Living Dead (1968):** A ragtag group of Pennsylvanians barricade themselves in an old farmhouse to remain safe from a horde of flesh-eating ghouls that are ravaging the East Coast of the United States.

☐ **The Omen (1976):** Mysterious deaths surround an American ambassador. Could the child that he is raising actually be the Antichrist? The Devil's own son? **Goof:** The priest's room is "lined with hundreds of crucifixes". In actuality they are just crosses, not crucifixes - crucifixes have an effigy of Jesus affixed to the cross.

☐ **The Others (2001):** A woman who lives in her darkened old family house with her two photosensitive children becomes convinced that the home is haunted.

☐ **Paranormal Activity (2007):** After moving into a suburban home, a couple becomes increasingly disturbed by a nightly demonic presence. **Fun Fact:** This is the most-profitable film of all-time. It cost $60,000 to make and $400,000 to market and then grossed over $89 million!

☐ **Peeping Tom (1960):** A young man murders women, using a movie camera to film their dying expressions of terror.

☐ **The Phantom of the Opera (1925):** A mad, disfigured composer seeks love with a lovely young opera singer.

☐ **Poltergeist (1982):** A family's home is haunted by a host of demonic ghosts. **Fun Fact:** During the scene where Robbie (Oliver Robins) is being strangled, the clown's arms became extremely tight and Robins started to choke. When he screamed out, "I can't breathe!" Steven Spielberg and Tobe Hooper thought that the boy was ad-libbing and just instructed him to look at the camera. When Spielberg saw Robins' face turning purple, he ran over and removed the clown's arms from Robins' neck. **Memorable Quote:** *"They're here!"*

☐ **Psycho (1960):** A Phoenix secretary embezzles forty thousand dollars from her employer's client, goes on the run, and checks into a remote motel run by a young man under the domination of his mother. **Fun Facts:** *Psycho* is the first U.S. film to feature a toilet flushing. **Goof:** Hitchcock's famous shower scene endures as a work of art unto itself, albeit one with a minor mistake. As Janet Leigh's character lies dead on the floor, her pupils are contracted when they're supposed to be dilated. After learning of the error, Hitchcock reportedly consulted with a handful of ophthalmologists, who recommended that he use belladonna eye drops when depicting murder victims. **Memorable Quote:** *"A boy's best friend is his mother."*

☐ **A Quiet Place (2018):** In a post-apocalyptic world, a family is forced to live in silence while hiding from monsters with ultra-sensitive hearing.

☐ **Rosemary's Baby (1968):** A young couple trying for a baby move into a fancy apartment surrounded by peculiar neighbors.

☐ **Saw (2004):** Two strangers awaken in a room with no recollection of how they got there, and soon discover they're pawns in a deadly game perpetrated by a notorious serial killer. **Fun Fact:** Worldwide ticket sales for the *Saw* franchise put it at just shy of a billion dollars, making it the highest earning horror franchise globally.

- ☐ **Scream (1996):** A year after the murder of her mother, a teenage girl is terrorized by a new killer, who targets the girl and her friends by using horror films as part of a deadly game. **Fun Fact:** It was originally titled *Scary Movie.*

- ☐ **The Shining (1980):** A family heads to an isolated hotel for the winter where a sinister presence influences the father to become violence, while his psychic son sees horrific forebodings from both past and future. **Fun Fact:** Stanley Kubrick would reportedly call Stephen King at 3:00 a.m. to ask him questions about *The Shining*. According to King, one famous exchange had the director ask the author, "Do you believe in God?" When he replied in the affirmative Kubrick yelled "I knew it!" and slammed the phone down. **Memorable Quote:** *"Here's Johnny!"*

- ☐ **The Sixth Sense (1999):** A boy who communicates with spirits seeks the help of a disheartened child psychologist. **Memorable Quote:** *"I see dead people."*

- ☐ **The Thing (1982):** A research team in Antarctica is hunted by a shape-shifting alien that assumes the appearance of its victims.

- ☐ **Tremors (1990):** Natives of a small isolated town defend themselves against strange underground creatures which are killing them one by one.

- ☐ **Village of the Damned (1960):** A small town's women give birth to unfriendly alien children posing as humans. **Goof:** The action takes place in the 1950s (some characters are wearing medal ribbons for the Korean War), but all of Major General Leighton's campaign ribbons predate 1939; he has no ribbons for World War II. He could have retired before 1939, but he would have been far too old to rejoin after the war.

- [ ] **Whatever Happened to Baby Jane? (1962):** A former child star torments her paraplegic sister in their decaying Hollywood mansion.

- [ ] **The Texas Chainsaw Massacre (1974):** Two siblings and three of their friends en route to visit their grandfather's grave in Texas fall victim to a family of cannibalistic psychopaths.

- [ ] **The Wicker Man (1973):** A puritan Police Sergeant arrives in a Scottish island village in search of a missing girl who the locals claim never existed. **My Two Cents:** One of the weirdest movies I have ever watched in my life, yet oddly arousing.

- [ ] **Zodiac (2007):** In the late 1960s/early 1970s, a San Francisco cartoonist becomes an amateur detective obsessed with tracking down the Zodiac Killer, an unidentified individual who terrorizes Northern California with a killing spree.

- [ ] **28 Days Later... (2002):** Four weeks after a mysterious, incurable virus spreads throughout the UK, a handful of survivors try to find sanctuary.

Musical

Musicals are a film genre in which songs by the characters are interwoven into the narrative, sometimes accompanied by dancing. The songs usually advance the plot or develop the film's characters, but in some cases, they serve merely as breaks in the storyline, often as elaborate "production numbers."

The musical film was a natural development of the stage musical after the emergence of sound film technology. Typically, the biggest difference between film and stage musicals is the use of lavish background scenery and locations that would be impractical in a theater. Musical films characteristically contain elements reminiscent of theater; performers often treat their song and dance numbers as if a live audience were watching. In a sense, the viewer becomes the diegetic audience, as the performer looks directly into the camera and performs to it.

☐ **All That Jazz (1979):** Director/choreographer Bob Fosse tells his own life story as he details the sordid career of Joe Gideon, a womanizing, drug-using dancer.

☐ **The Band Wagon (1953):** A pretentiously artistic director is hired for a new Broadway musical and changes it beyond recognition.

☐ **The Blues Brothers (1980):** Jake Blues, just released from prison, puts together his old band to save the Catholic home where he and his brother Elwood were raised. **Goof:** While chasing the Blues Brothers, the troopers state that they are southbound on Highway 47. Illinois Rt 47 is west of Chicago and does not enter the city limits of Chicago.

☐ **Bohemian Rhapsody (2018):** The story of the legendary British rock band Queen and lead singer Freddie Mercury, leading up to their famous performance at Live Aid (1985).

☐ **Cabaret (1972):** A female girlie club entertainer in Weimar Republic era Berlin romances two men while the Nazi Party rises to power around them.

☐ **Dirty Dancing (1987):** Spending the summer at a Catskills resort with her family, Frances "Baby" Houseman falls in love with the camp's dance instructor, Johnny Castle. **Memorable Quote:** *"Nobody puts Baby in a corner."*

☐ **Easter Parade (1948):** A nightclub performer hires a naive chorus girl to become his new dance partner to make his former partner jealous and to prove he can make any partner a star.

☐ **Fame (1980):** A chronicle of the lives of several teenagers who attend a New York high school for students gifted in the performing arts.

☐ **Footloose (1984):** A city teenager moves to a small town where rock music and dancing have been banned, and his rebellious spirit shakes up the populace. **Fun Fact:** Loosely based on events that took place in the small, rural, and extremely religious farming town of Elmore City, Oklahoma in 1978. Dancing had been banned for nearly ninety years, until a group of high school teenagers challenged it.

☐ **Funny Face (1957):** An impromptu fashion shoot at a book store brings about a new fashion model discovery in the shop clerk.

☐ **Funny Girl (1968):** The life of Fanny Brice, famed comedienne and entertainer of the early 1900s. We see her rise to fame as a Ziegfeld girl, subsequent career, and her personal life. **Memorable Quote:** *"Hello, gorgeous."*

☐ **The Gang's All Here (1943):** A soldier falls for a chorus girl and then experiences trouble when he is posted to the Pacific.

☐ **Gentlemen Prefer Blondes (1953):** Showgirls Lorelei Lee and Dorothy Shaw travel to Paris, pursued by a private detective hired by the suspicious father of Lorelei's fiancé.

☐ **Gold Diggers of 1933 (1933):** A wealthy composer rescues unemployed Broadway performers with a new play. **Fun Fact:** During rehearsals of "We're in the Money", Ginger Rogers began goofing off and singing in pig Latin. Studio executive Darryl F. Zanuck overheard her, and suggested she do it for real in the movie.

☐ **Grease (1978):** Good girl Sandy and greaser Danny had fallen in love over the summer. When they discover they're now in the same high school, will they be able to rekindle their romance? **Best Song:** "You're the One that I Want" **Second:** "Summer Nights"

☐ **The Greatest Showman (2017):** Celebrates the birth of show business and tells of a visionary who rose from nothing to create a spectacle that became a worldwide sensation. **Best Song:** "This is Me"

☐ **Guys and Dolls (1955):** In New York, a gambler is challenged to take a cold female missionary to Havana, but they fall for each other, and the bet has a hidden motive to finance a crap game.

☐ **Hairspray (1988):** A 'pleasantly plump' teenager teaches 1962 Baltimore a thing or two about integration after landing a spot on a local TV dance show. **Fun Fact:** Ricki Lake began rapidly losing weight due to the intense dance lessons she had to take for the film. She reportedly had to "eat like crazy" in order to stay plump.

☐ **Hamilton (2020):** The real life of one of America's foremost founding fathers and first Secretary of the Treasury, Alexander Hamilton. Captured live on Broadway from the Richard Rodgers Theater with the original Broadway cast.

☐ **A Hard Day's Night (1964):** Over two "typical" days in the life of The Beatles, the boys struggle to keep themselves and Sir Paul McCartney's mischievous grandfather in check while preparing for a live television performance. **Fun Fact:** The name of the band isn't mentioned once in The Beatles' first feature, *A Hard Day's Night*.

☐ **Hello, Dolly! (1969):** Matchmaker Dolly Levi travels to Yonkers to find a partner for "half-a-millionaire" Horace Vandergelder, convincing his niece, his niece's intended, and his two clerks to travel to New York City along the way.

☐ **High Society (1956):** A spoiled heiress must choose among three suitors: her jazz musician ex-husband, a stuffy businessman and an undercover tabloid reporter.

☐ **The King and I (1956):** A widow accepts a job as a live-in governess to the King of Siam's children. **Goof:** The map of the world prominently visible in the classroom shows parts of the Arctic and Antarctic regions that hadn't yet been explored or mapped in 1862.

☐ **La La Land (2016):** While navigating their careers in Los Angeles, a pianist and an actress fall in love while attempting to reconcile their aspirations for the future.

☐ **The Last Waltz (1978):** A film account and presentation of the final concert of The Band.

☐ **Les Misérables (2012):** In 19th-century France, Jean Valjean, who for decades has been hunted by the ruthless policeman Javert after breaking parole, agrees to care for a factory worker's daughter. The decision changes their lives forever. **Fun Fact:** Hugh Jackman lost considerable weight and went 36 hours without water, causing him to lose water weight around his eyes and cheeks, giving him the gaunt appearance of a prisoner. He also grew a real scraggly beard for scenes of Valjean as a prisoner, though mercifully they were shot first in production and he could shave and return to his usual weight for scenes playing Valjean as a wealthy man.

☐ **Little Shop of Horrors (1986):** A nerdy florist finds his chance for success and romance with the help of a giant man-eating plant who demands to be fed.

☐ **Meet Me in St. Louis (1944):** Young love and childish fears highlight a year in the life of a turn-of-the-century family.

☐ **Moulin Rouge! (2001):** A poet falls for a beautiful courtesan whom a jealous duke covets. **Fun Fact:** The necklace worn by Nicole Kidman was made of real diamonds and platinum and was the most expensive piece of jewelry ever specifically made for a film. The Stefano Canturi necklace was made with 1,308 diamonds, weighing a total of 134 carats and was worth an estimated U.S. $1 million. **Fun Fact:** Filming was halted for two weeks in November 1999 after Nicole Kidman fractured two ribs and injured her knee while rehearsing a dance routine for the film. Many of the scenes where she is seen only from the chest up, including "a real actress," were shot while she was in a wheelchair.

☐ **New York, New York (1977):** An egotistical saxophonist and a young lounge singer meet on VJ Day and embark upon a strained and rocky romance, even as their careers begin a long, uphill climb.

☐ **A Night at the Opera (1935):** A sly business manager and two wacky friends of two opera singers help them achieve success while humiliating their stuffy and snobbish enemies.

☐ **Oklahoma! (1955):** In Oklahoma, several farmers, cowboys and a traveling salesman compete for the romantic favors of various local ladies. **Fun Fact:** Tone deaf, Gloria Grahame, who played Ado Annie, sang without dubbing, which required that her songs to be edited together from recordings made almost literally note by note.

☐ **On the Town (1949):** Three sailors wreak havoc as they search for love during a whirlwind 24-hour leave in New York City.

☐ **Pal Joey (1957):** Joey Evans' a charming, handsome, funny, talented a-1st class, A-N°.1 - heel. When Joey meets the former chorus girl and now is the rich widow, Vera Simpson, the pair of lecherous souls seem made for each other. **Memorable Quote:** *"After all, two years is a long time between... drinks."*

☐ **The Red Shoes (1948):** A young ballet dancer is torn between the man she loves and her pursuit to become a prima ballerina.

☐ **Rocketman (2019):** A musical fantasy about the fantastical human story of Elton John's breakthrough years. **Best Song:** "I'm Still Standing"

☐ **The Rocky Horror Picture Show (1975):** A newly engaged couple have a breakdown in an isolated area and must pay a call to the bizarre residence of Dr. Frank N. Furter. **Best Song:** "Time Warp" **My Two Cents:** I want to go to one of the showings where you dress up as a character, and they reenact it.

☐ **Saturday Night Fever (1977):** Anxious about his future after high school, a 19-year-old Italian-American from Brooklyn tries to escape the harsh reality of his bleak family life by dominating the dance floor at the local disco.

☐ **Singin' in the Rain (1952):** A silent film production company and cast make a difficult transition to sound. **Goof:** The most famous scene in this acclaimed musical appropriately features Gene Kelly singing and tap-dancing in the rain. Keen observers might notice that the sound of tapping doesn't always match up to the movements of his feet. In fact, listen closely enough and one might hear the sound of tapping even after Kelly's stopped dancing altogether.

☐ **Straight Outta Compton (2015):** The rap group NWA emerges from the mean streets of Compton in Los Angeles, California, in the mid-1980s and revolutionizes Hip Hop culture with their music and tales about life in the hood.

☐ **A Star is Born (1954):** A film star helps a young singer and actress find fame, even as age and alcoholism send his own career on a downward spiral. **My Two Cents:** This is my favorite out of all four *A Star is Born* movies.

☐ **Strike Up the Band (1940):** Jimmy Connors and his girlfriend want to take part in Paul Whiteman's high school bands contest, but they cannot afford the fare. But per chance they meet Paul

Whiteman in person and are able to convince him that their band is good enough, so he lends them the money. But then one of their friends becomes seriously ill and has to be carried to a hospital by plane, and they have to use Whiteman's money for this.

- ☐ **South Pacific (1958):** On a South Pacific island during World War II, love blooms between a young nurse and a secretive Frenchman who's being courted for a dangerous military mission.

- ☐ **Top Hat (1935):** An American dancer comes to Britain and falls for a model whom he initially annoyed, but she mistakes him for his goofy producer. **Fun Fact:** The first time Fred Astaire and Ginger Rogers had a screenplay written specifically for them.

- ☐ **Viva Las Vegas (1964):** A race car driver preparing for the Grand Prix, wiles his time in Las Vegas working as a waiter to pay for his new engine. Soon, he strikes up a romance with a beautiful young woman.

- ☐ **Walk the Line (2005):** A chronicle of country music legend Johnny Cash's life, from his early days on an Arkansas cotton farm to his rise to fame with Sun Records in Memphis, where he recorded alongside Elvis Presley, Jerry Lee Lewis, and Carl Perkins. **Best Song:** "Ring of Fire"

- ☐ **Whiplash (2014):** A promising young drummer enrolls at a cut-throat music conservatory where his dreams of greatness are mentored by an instructor who will stop at nothing to realize a student's potential.

- ☐ **The Wizard of Oz (1939):** Dorothy Gale is swept away from her home in Kansas to the magical Land of Oz in a tornado and embarks on a quest with her new friends to see the Wizard who can help her return home and help her friends as well. **Misquote:** "Toto, we're not in Kansas anymore." **Actual Quote:** "Toto, *I've a feeling* we're not in Kansas anymore." **Fun Fact:** The snow falling down was actually asbestos. **Goof:** When Dorothy and the Scarecrow meet the Tin Man for the first time, they apply oil to his rusty joints so that he can move. There's just one problem: tin doesn't rust. **Memorable Quote:** *"There's no place like home."* **Memorable Quote:** *"I'll get you, my pretty, and your little dog, too!"*

☐ **Woodstock (1970):** Oscar-winning musical chronicle that brilliantly captures the three-day rock concert and celebration of peace and love that became a capstone for the Sixties.

☐ **Yankee Doodle Dandy (1942):** The life of the renowned musical composer, playwright, actor, dancer, and singer George M. Cohan. **Memorable Quote:** *"My mother thanks you. My father thanks you. My sister thanks you. And I thank you."*

☐ **You Were Never Lovelier (1942):** In Buenos Aires, a man who has decreed that his daughters must marry in order of age allows an American dancer to perform at his club under the condition that he play suitor to his second-oldest daughter.

☐ **42nd Street (1933):** When the leading lady of a Broadway musical breaks her ankle, she is replaced by a young unknown actress, who becomes the star of the show. **Memorable Quote:** *"Sawyer, you're going out a youngster, but you've got to come back a star!"*

Romance

This genre is why I have such an unrealistic view about relationships. I think that sums up everything in my life. I want a happy ending, I am getting there, but I want him to jump through hoops to save me and that is just not how relationships work in the real world. Although, however, how he got me is a beautiful tale in itself. You can have a happy ending, just not how you will expect it. Romance movies don't tell the heartaches of real life and real-life situations as in our everyday lives and how they can be boring and repetitive.

A lot of these movies are so beautiful and give me all the feels. Then I threw in some to make it a good number, even though I am not sure if they fit on this list. Some I picked because of the fan base and not necessarily my personal preference. Side Note: It's probably not an even number anymore.

- ☐ **About a Boy (2002):** A cynical, immature young man is taught how to act like a grown-up by a little boy.
- ☐ **Adam's Rib (1949):** Domestic and professional tensions mount when a husband-and-wife work as opposing lawyers in a case involving a woman who shot her husband. **Fun Fact:** Inspired by the real-life story of husband-and-wife lawyers William Dwight Whitney and Dorothy Whitney, who represented Raymond Massey and his ex-wife Adrienne Allen in their divorce. After the Massey divorce was over, the Whitneys divorced each other and married the respective Masseys.
- ☐ **Age of Innocence (1993):** A tale of nineteenth-century New York high society in which a young lawyer falls in love with a woman separated from her husband, while he is engaged to the woman's cousin.

☐ **An Affair to Remember (1957):** A couple falls in love and agrees to meet in six months at the Empire State Building - but will it happen? **My Two Cents:** One of my favorite romance movies of all time.

☐ **As Good as It Gets (1997):** A single mother and waitress, a misanthropic author, and a gay artist form an unlikely friendship after the artist is assaulted in a robbery. **Memorable Quote:** *"You make me want to be a better man."*

☐ **The Awful Truth (1937):** Unfounded suspicions lead a married couple to begin divorce proceedings, whereupon they start undermining each other's attempts to find new romance.

☐ **Barefoot in the Park (1967):** Paul, a conservative young lawyer, marries the vivacious Corie. Their highly passionate relationship descends into comical discord in a five-flight New York City walk-up apartment.

☐ **Before Sunrise (1995):** A young man and woman meet on a train in Europe, and wind-up spending one evening together in Vienna. Unfortunately, both know that this will probably be their only night together. **Memorable Quote:** *"I like to feel his eyes on me when I look away."*

☐ **Before Sunset (2004):** Nine years after Jesse and Celine first met, they encounter each other again on the French leg of Jesse's book tour. **Full disclosure:** I haven't seen this or the prequel, but they are both in the top 250 on IMDB.com.

☐ **The Best Man (1999):** Just before his best friend's wedding, the life of a Chicago writer becomes crazy when his best friend guesses that his new book's story is based on his bride's fervent past.

☐ **The Big Sick (2017):** Pakistan-born comedian Kumail Nanjiani and grad student Emily Gardner fall in love but struggle as their cultures clash. When Emily contracts a mysterious illness, Kumail finds himself forced to face her feisty parents, his family's expectations, and his true feelings.

☐ **Breakfast at Tiffany's (1961):** A young New York socialite becomes interested in a young man who has moved into her apartment building, but her past threatens to get in the way. **Fun Fact:** Audrey Hepburn's salary for the film was $750,000, making her the highest paid actress per film at the time.

☐ **The Break-Up (2006):** In a bid to keep their luxurious condo from their significant other, a couple's break-up proceeds to get uglier and nastier by the moment.

☐ **Brown Sugar (2002):** Friends since childhood, a magazine editor and a hip-hop record executive stumble into romantic territory.

☐ **Brief Encounter (1945):** Meeting a stranger in a railway station, a woman is tempted to cheat on her husband. **Goof:** Carnforth Station has had its name board covered and replaced with a big sign reading Milford Junction, but the smaller platform notices (behind Laura when Alec tells her about the job in South Africa) still show the next train's destinations as Hellifield, Skipton, Bradford and Leeds.

☐ **Camille (1936):** A Parisian courtesan must choose between the young man who loves her and the callous baron who wants her, even as her own health begins to fail.

☐ **Carol (2015):** An aspiring photographer develops an intimate relationship with an older woman in 1950s New York.

☐ **To Catch a Thief (1955):** A retired jewel thief sets out to prove his innocence after being suspected of returning to his former occupation. **Memorable Quote:** *"Not only did I enjoy that kiss last night, I was awed by its efficiency."*

☐ **Chasing Amy (1997):** Holden and Banky are comic book artists. Everything's going good for them until they meet Alyssa, also a comic book artist. Holden falls for her, but his hopes are crushed when he finds out she's a lesbian.

☐ **Crazy/Beautiful (2001):** At Pacific Palisades High, a poor Latino falls hard for a troubled girl from an affluent neighborhood.

☐ **Crazy Rich Asians (2018):** This contemporary romantic comedy, based on a global bestseller, follows native New Yorker Rachel Chu to Singapore to meet her boyfriend's family. **Fun Fact:** Most of Awkwafina's lines as Peik Lin Goh were improvised.

☐ **Crazy, Stupid, Love (2011):** A middle-aged husband's life changes dramatically when his wife asks him for a divorce. He seeks to rediscover his manhood with the help of a newfound friend, Jacob, learning to pick up girls at bars.

☐ **Definitely, Maybe (2008):** A political consultant tries to explain his impending divorce and past relationships to his 11-year-old daughter.

☐ **Deliver Us from Eva (2003):** Eva doesn't let her 3 sisters' men push them around. She's always butting in. How to pacify Eva? Find her a man. The men pay a playboy to be that man. The problem is - he falls in love with Eva. **Fun Fact:** Second *Taming of the Shrew* adaptation that Gabrielle Union is in. The first one was *10 Things I Hate About You* (1999).

☐ **The English Patient (1996):** At the close of World War II, a young nurse tends to a badly-burned plane crash victim. His past is shown in flashbacks, revealing an involvement in a fateful love affair.

☐ **Enough Said (2013):** A divorced woman who decides to pursue the man she's interested in learns he's her new friend's ex-husband.

☐ **The Fabulous Baker Boys (1989):** The lives of two struggling musicians, who happen to be brothers, inevitably change when they team up with a beautiful, up-and-coming singer. **Goof:** When Jack goes to Frank's house, he is dropped off by a cab from the "Bay City Cab Co." However, the movie takes place in Seattle, not San Francisco (the Bay City).

☐ **Forgetting Sarah Marshall (2008):** Devastated Peter takes a Hawaiian vacation in order to deal with the recent break-up with his TV star girlfriend, Sarah. Little does he know, Sarah's traveling to the same resort as her ex - and she's bringing along her new boyfriend.

☐ **The French Lieutenant's Woman (1981):** Anna and Mike portray two characters in a film set in 19th century England who fall in love despite the fact that Mike's character is engaged.

☐ **The Ghost and Mrs. Muir (1947):** In 1900, a young widow finds her seaside cottage is haunted and forms a unique relationship with the ghost. **Fun Fact:** The word "muir" means "sea" in Scots Gaelic. Many times sailors are said to have been "married" to the sea, or that the only woman they ever loved was the sea.

☐ **Garden State (2004):** A quietly troubled young man returns home for his mother's funeral after being estranged from his family for a decade.

☐ **Green Card (1990):** A man wanting to stay in the US enters into a marriage of convenience, but it turns into more than that.

☐ **High Fidelity (2000):** Rob, a record store owner and compulsive list maker, recounts his top five breakups, including the one in progress. **Memorable Quote:** *"Sometimes I got so bored of trying to touch her breast that I would try to touch her between her legs. It was like trying to borrow a dollar, getting turned down, and asking for 50 grand instead."*

☐ **Hitch (2005):** A smooth-talking man falls for a hardened columnist while helping a shy accountant woo a beautiful heiress. **Best Song:** "Now that We Found Love"

☐ **Hope Floats (1998):** Birdee Calvert must choose between her morals and her heart after her husband divorces her and a charming young man, who her daughter disapproves of, comes back into her life.

☐ **How Stella Got Her Groove Back (1998):** Stella is a highly successful, forty-something San Francisco stock broker who is persuaded by her colorful New York girlfriend Delilah to take a well-deserved, first-class vacation to Jamaica. **Fun Fact:** The movie was based on a book by Terry McMillan who wrote about her own life and marriage to Jamaican Jonathan Plummer in 1998. She was in her late forties and he in his early twenties. In December 2004, Plummer told McMillan that he was gay, and in March 2005, she filed for divorce. He essentially only married her so he could leave Jamaica and gain American citizenship.

☐ **How to Marry a Millionaire (1953):** Three women set out to find eligible millionaires to marry, but find true love in the process.

☐ **How to Lose a Guy in 10 Days (2003):** Benjamin Barry is an advertising executive and ladies' man who, to win a big campaign, bets that he can make a woman fall in love with him in 10 days.

☐ **If Beale Street Could Talk (2018):** A young woman embraces her pregnancy while she and her family set out to prove her childhood friend and lover innocent of a crime he didn't commit. **Memorable Quote:** *"I don't want to sound foolish, but remember love is what brought you here. And if you've trusted love this far, don't panic now. Trust it all the way."*

☐ **I Feel Pretty (2018):** A woman struggling with insecurity wakes from a fall believing she is the most beautiful and capable woman on the planet. Her new confidence empowers her to live fearlessly, but what happens when she realizes her appearance never changed?

☐ **If Lucy Fell (1996):** Two NYC roomies have a pact to jump off Brooklyn Bridge, if they haven't found life partners before she's 30. That's less than a month away. **My Two Cents:** I included this because for some odd reason it is one of my mother's favorite romantic comedies.

☐ **It's Complicated (2009):** When attending their son's college graduation, a couple reignite the spark in their relationship. But the complicated fact is they're divorced and he's remarried.

☐ **Just Friends (2005):** While visiting his hometown during Christmas, a man comes face-to-face with his old high school crush whom he was best friends with -- a woman whose rejection of him turned him into a ferocious womanizer.

☐ **Knocked Up (2007):** For fun-loving party animal Ben Stone, the last thing he ever expected was for his one-night stand to show up on his doorstep eight weeks later to tell him she's pregnant with his child. **Fun Fact:** Judd Apatow originally planned to use real footage of a woman giving birth for the delivery scene. He had to change it because child labor laws required the infant to have a work permit.

☐ **The Lady Eve (1941):** A trio of classy card sharps targets the socially awkward heir to brewery millions for his money, until one of them falls in love with him.

☐ **Love, Guaranteed (2020):** To save her small law firm, earnest lawyer Susan takes a high-paying case from Nick, a charming new client who wants to sue a dating website that guarantees love. But as the case heats up, so do Susan and Nick's feelings for each other.

☐ **Love Story (1970):** A boy and a girl from different backgrounds fall in love regardless of their upbringing - and then tragedy strikes. **Memorable Quote:** *"Love means never having to say you're sorry."*

☐ **Loving (2016):** The story of Richard and Mildred Loving, a couple whose arrest for interracial marriage in 1960s Virginia began a legal battle that would end with the Supreme Court's historic 1967 decision.

☐ **Me Before You (2016):** A girl in a small town forms an unlikely bond with a recently-paralyzed man she's taking care of.

☐ **Much Ado About Nothing (1993):** Young lovers Hero and Claudio, soon to wed, conspire to get verbal sparring partners and confirmed singles Benedick and Beatrice to wed as well. **Goof:** An accordion appears at the masquerade ball. This instrument was not invented until 1822.

☐ **Muriel's Wedding (1994):** A young social outcast in Australia steals money from her parents to finance a vacation where she hopes to find happiness, and perhaps love.

☐ **My Best Friend's Wedding (1997):** When a woman's long-time friend reveals he's engaged, she realizes she loves him herself and sets out to get him, only days before the wedding.

☐ **My Big Fat Greek Wedding (2002):** A young Greek woman falls in love with a non-Greek and struggles to get her family to accept him while she comes to terms with her heritage and cultural identity. **Fun Fact:** Tom Hanks' wife, Rita Wilson, saw the play and recommended that her husband produce a movie version. In an interview with the German magazine *Cinema*, Nia Vardalos mentioned that she hung up when Hanks called because she did not believe it was really him.

☐ **Ninotchka (1939):** A stern Russian woman sent to Paris on official business finds herself attracted to a man who represents everything she is supposed to detest.

☐ **No Strings Attached (2011):** A guy and girl try to keep their relationship strictly physical, but it's not long before they learn that they want something more.

☐ **The Notebook (2004):** A poor yet passionate young man falls in love with a rich young woman, giving her a sense of freedom, but they are soon separated because of their social differences. **Fun Fact:** According to Nick Cassavetes, Ryan Gosling and Rachel McAdams did not get along at first and Gosling tried to have McAdams replaced. To improve the relationship between the leads, director Nick Cassavetes staged an intervention by bringing them into a room where they could air all the grievances they had with each other and work something out. They soon patched over their differences, enough to become a real-life couple for some time.

☐ **Notting Hill (1999):** The life of a simple bookshop owner changes when he meets the most famous film star in the world. **My Favorite**

Line: *"I'm also just a girl, standing in front of a boy, asking him to love her."*

☐ **Now, Voyager (1942):** A frumpy spinster blossoms under therapy and becomes an elegant, independent woman. **My Favorite Line:** *"Oh, Jerry, don't let's ask for the moon. We have the stars."*

☐ **An Officer and a Gentleman (1982):** A young man must complete his work at a Navy Officer Candidate School to become an aviator, with the help of a tough Gunnery Sergeant and his new girlfriend.

☐ **Overboard (1987):** A cruel but beautiful heiress mocks and cheats a hired carpenter. When she gets amnesia after an accident, he decides to introduce her to regular life by convincing her they're husband and wife.

☐ **Palm Springs (2020):** Stuck in a time loop, two wedding guests develop a budding romance while living the same day over and over again. **Goof:** Toward the end of the movie when Nyles says "dot, dot, dot" in his speech. Sarah corrects him and says, "It's called an ellipses." 'Ellipses' is the plural form of ellipsis. 'Ellipsis' is the singular noun describing a punctuation mark represented by three dots.

☐ **The Philadelphia Story (1940):** When a rich woman's ex-husband and a tabloid-type reporter turn up just before her planned remarriage, she begins to learn the truth about herself.

☐ **Portrait of a Lady on Fire (2019):** On an isolated island in Brittany at the end of the eighteenth century, a female painter is obliged to paint a wedding portrait of a young woman.

☐ **Pretty Woman (1990):** A businessman hires a beautiful prostitute for a short-term romp, but ends up falling for her. **Fun Fact:** Edward (Richard Gere) snapping the necklace case down on Vivian's (Julia Roberts) fingers, was improvised by Gere, and Roberts's reaction (laughter) was totally natural. The filmmakers liked it so much, they decided to leave it in.

☐ **Pride and Prejudice (2005):** Sparks fly when spirited Elizabeth Bennet meets single, rich, and proud Mr. Darcy. But Mr. Darcy reluctantly finds himself falling in love with a woman beneath his class. Can each overcome their own pride and prejudice?

☐ **The Proposal (2009):** A pushy boss forces her young assistant to marry her in order to keep her visa status in the U.S. and avoid deportation to Canada.

☐ **P.S. I Love You (2007):** A young widow discovers that her late husband has left her 10 messages intended to help ease her pain and start a new life. **Fun Fact:** During the filming of a strip sequence, Gerard Butler's suspenders hit Hilary Swank on the forehead. She received a cut and had to be taken to a hospital, where she received several stitches.

☐ **The Quiet Man (1952):** A retired American boxer returns to the village of his birth in Ireland, where he falls for a spirited redhead, whose brother is contemptuous of their union.

☐ **Random Harvest (1942):** An amnesiac World War I veteran falls in love with a music hall star, only to suffer an accident which restores his original memories but erases his post-war life. **My Two Cents:** Another one of my favorite romance movies that I would love to be remade today.

☐ **Reality Bites (1994):** A documentary filmmaker and her fellow Generation X graduates face life after college, looking for work and love in Houston.

☐ **Romancing the Stone (1984):** A mousy romance novelist sets off for Colombia to ransom her kidnapped sister, and soon finds herself in the middle of a dangerous adventure hunting for treasure with a mercenary rogue.

☐ **Roman Holiday (1953):** A bored and sheltered princess escapes her guardians and falls in love with an American newsman in Rome. **Fun Fact:** After filming, Gregory Peck informed the producers that, as Audrey Hepburn was certainly going to win an

Oscar (for this, her first major role), they had better put her name above the title. They did and she did.

☐ **Romeo and Juliet (1996):** Shakespeare's famous play is updated to the hip modern suburb of Verona still retaining its original dialogue.

☐ **Sabrina (1954):** A playboy becomes interested in the daughter of his family's chauffeur, but it's his more serious brother who would be the better man for her.

☐ **Save the Last Dance (2001):** A white midwestern girl moves to Chicago, where her new boyfriend is a black teen from the South Side with a rough, semi-criminal past. **Goof:** Juilliard is misspelled as "Julliard" on the sign announcing auditions.

☐ **Serendipity (2001):** A couple search for each other years after the night they first met, fell in love, and separated, convinced that one day they'd end up together.

☐ **Set It Up (2018):** Two corporate executive assistants hatch a plan to match-make their two bosses.

☐ **The Seven-Year Itch (1955):** When his family goes away for the summer, a hitherto faithful husband with an overactive imagination is tempted by a beautiful neighbor. **Fun Fact:** Marilyn Monroe's iconic white dress set a record when it was auctioned for $4.6 million in June 2011 (rising to $5.5 million after taxes and fees were included), quintupling the previous record for a movie costume ($923,000 for Audrey Hepburn's "little black dress" from *Breakfast at Tiffany's*). **Fun Fact:** Billy Wilder preferred shooting in black and white, but Marilyn Monroe's contract with Fox called for all of her movies to be shot in color. Monroe always thought that she looked far more attractive and glamorous in color than in black and white.

☐ **The Shop Around the Corner (1940):** Two employees at a gift shop can barely stand each other, without realizing that they are falling in love through the post as each other's anonymous pen pal.

☐ **Sleepless in Seattle (1993):** A recently widowed man's son calls a radio talk-show in an attempt to find his father a partner. Is there anything better than a Tom Hanks/Meg Ryan movie, I mean, honestly? **Memorable Quote:** *"Destiny is something we've invented because we can't stand the fact that everything that happens is accidental."*

☐ **Sliding Doors (1998):** A London woman's love life and career both hinge, unknown to her, on whether or not she catches a train. We see it both ways, in parallel. **My Two Cents:** One of the most underrated romantic comedies of all-time and that is why it is on this list. I love the concept that has not been utilized enough.

☐ **Splash (1984):** A young man is reunited with a mermaid who saved him from drowning as a boy. He falls in love with her, not knowing who or what she is.

☐ **Sweet Home Alabama (2002):** A young woman who's reinvented herself as a New York City socialite must return home to Alabama to obtain a divorce from her husband, after seven years of separation.

☐ **Sweet November (2001):** A workaholic executive and an unconventional woman agree to a personal relationship for a short period. In this short period, she changes his life. **My Two Cents:** One of my best friend's favorite movies, so I included it. Yep, I have yet to watch it.

☐ **The Time Traveler's Wife (2009):** A Chicago librarian has a gene that causes him to involuntarily time travel, creating complications in his marriage.

☐ **Think Like a Man (2012):** Four friends conspire to turn the tables on their women when they discover the ladies have been using Steve Harvey's relationship advice against them.

☐ **Twilight (2008):** When Bella Swan moves to a small town in the Pacific Northwest, she falls in love with Edward Cullen, a mysterious classmate who reveals himself to be a 108-year-old vampire. **Fun Fact:** For the role of Edward Cullen, Robert Pattinson flew from England to director Catherine Hardwicke's house to audition. There, he and Kristen Stewart, who was already cast as Bella Swan, rehearsed the "Love Scene"/"Meadow Scene" on Hardwicke's own bed.

☐ **The Ugly Truth (2009):** An uptight television producer takes control of a morning show segment on modern relationships hosted by a misogynistic man.

☐ **Waiting to Exhale (1995):** Based on Terry McMillan's novel, this film follows four very different African-American women and their relationships with men.

☐ **Waterloo Bridge (1940):** During World War I, believing her fiancé to be dead, a young ballerina loses her job and is forced to turn to prostitution. **Fun Fact:** Of her films, this was Vivien Leigh's personal favorite. Yes, it beats out *Gone with the Wind!*

☐ **The Way We Were (1973):** Two disparate people have a wonderful romance, but their political views and convictions drive them apart.

☐ **The Wedding Date (2005):** Single-girl anxiety causes Kat Ellis to hire a male escort to pose as her boyfriend at her sister's wedding. Her plan, an attempt to dupe her ex-fiancé, who dumped her a couple years prior, proves to be her undoing.

☐ **The Wedding Singer (1998):** Robbie, a singer, and Julia, a waitress, are both engaged, but to the wrong people. Fortune intervenes to help them discover each other. **Best Song:** "You Spin Me Round (Like a Record)"

☐ **When a Man Loves a Woman (1994):** The seemingly perfect relationship between a man and his wife is tested as a result of her alcoholism.

☐ **When Harry Met Sally (1989):** Harry and Sally have known each other for years and are very good friends, but they fear sex would ruin the friendship. **Memorable Quote:** *"I'll have what she's having."* **My Favorite Line:** *"When you realize you want to spend the rest of your life with somebody, you want the rest of your life to start as soon as possible."*

☐ **When We First Met (2018):** Noah meets Avery at a Halloween party and falls in love but gets friend-zoned. 3 years later, she's engaged to someone else. Noah returns in a time machine to fix things.

☐ **While You Were Sleeping (1995):** A hopeless romantic Chicago Transit Authority token collector is mistaken for the fiancée of a coma patient. **My Two Cents:** My favorite Sandra Bullock performance, and one of my favorite modern-day romance movies.

☐ **Wuthering Heights (1939):** A servant in the house of Wuthering Heights tells a traveler the unfortunate tale of lovers Cathy and Heathcliff.

☐ **You've Got Mail (1998):** Book superstore magnate, Joe Fox and independent book shop owner, Kathleen Kelly falls in love in the anonymity of the Internet both blissfully unaware that he's trying to put her out of business.

☐ **9 1/2 weeks (1986):** A woman becomes involved with a man she barely knows. Complications develop during their sexual escapades. **Fun Fact:** Kim Basinger owns 14 hours of deleted scenes that MGM thought were very psychologically damaging to people. The footage has never been made available for public viewing, even in the Director's Cut DVD edition.

☐ **10 (1979):** A Hollywood composer goes through a mid-life crisis and becomes infatuated with a sexy, newly married woman. **My Two Cents:** Just cause of the famous water scene of Bo Derek, I decided to include it.

☐ **500 Days of Summer (2009):** An offbeat romantic comedy about a woman who doesn't believe true love exists, and the young man who falls for her.

Science Fiction/Fantasy

Science fiction (or sci-fi) is a film genre that uses speculative, fictional science-based depictions of phenomena that are not fully accepted by mainstream science, such as extraterrestrial lifeforms, alien worlds, extrasensory perception and time travel, along with futuristic elements such as spacecraft, robots, cyborgs, interstellar travel or other technologies. Science fiction films have often been used to focus on political or social issues, and to explore philosophical issues like the human condition.

The genre has existed since the early years of silent cinema, when Georges Melies' *A Trip to the Moon* (1902) employed trick photography effects. The next major example (first in feature length in the genre) was the film *Metropolis* (1927). From the 1930s to the 1950s, the genre consisted mainly of low-budget B movies. After Stanley Kubrick's landmark *2001: A Space Odyssey* (1968), the science fiction film genre was taken more seriously. In the late 1970s, big-budget science fiction films filled with special effects became popular with audiences after the success of *Star Wars* (1977) and paved the way for the blockbuster hits of subsequent decades.

Screenwriter and scholar Eric R. Williams identifies Science Fiction Films as one of eleven super-genres in his screenwriters' taxonomy, claiming that all feature length narrative films can be classified by these super-genres. The other ten super-genres are Action, Crime, Fantasy, Horror, Romance, Slice of Life, Sports, Thriller, War and Western.

This, again, comes from the definition from Wikipedia, as most in this book. I wish I could write a good sci-fi, and here comes the conspiracy theorist in me, but some do feel like they knew the future or know about what is going to happen as in the human psyche such as *The Matrix.* I am a very spiritual person and I definitely believe we are not alone on this universe and that there are higher intelligent beings than we are, just look at the pyramids in Egypt! Those were not built by humans. YouTube some videos on that shit, it's crazy!

☐ **A.I. Artificial Intelligence (2001):** A highly advanced robotic boy longs to become "real" so that he can regain the love of his human mother.

☐ **Alien Franchise (1979):** After a space merchant vessel receives an unknown transmission as a distress call, one of the crew is attacked by a mysterious life form and they soon realize that its life cycle has merely begun. **Misquote:** "Stay away from her, you bitch." **Actual Quote:** "*Get* away from her, you bitch."

☐ **Atomic Blonde (2017):** An undercover MI6 agent is sent to Berlin during the Cold War to investigate the murder of a fellow agent and recover a missing list of double agents.

☐ **Avatar (2009):** A paraplegic Marine dispatched to the moon Pandora on a unique mission becomes torn between following his orders and protecting the world he feels is his home. **Fun Fact:** James Cameron was convinced that CGI effects had progressed enough to make this film when he saw Gollum in The Lord of the Rings: The Two Towers (2002). **Fun Fact:** Director James Cameron, known for being tough on set, allegedly kept a nail-gun on set that he would use to nail cell phones, that had the misfortune of ringing, to a wall above the exit sign. **Fun Fact:** The cigarette smoked by Sigourney Weaver in *Avatar* is completely CGI.

☐ **The Avengers Franchise (2012):** Earth's mightiest heroes must come together and learn to fight as a team if they are going to stop the mischievous Loki and his alien army from enslaving humanity.

☐ **Back to the Future Franchise (1985):** Marty McFly, a 17-year-old high school student, is accidentally sent thirty years into the past in a time-traveling DeLorean invented by his close friend, the eccentric scientist Doc Brown. **Fun Fact:** Disney turned down the chance to make *Back to the Future* claiming the mother/son relationship was too risqué. **Memorable Quote:** *"Roads? Where we're going, we don't need roads."*

- ☐ **Batman Franchise (1989):** The Dark Knight of Gotham City begins his war on crime with his first major enemy being Jack Napier, a criminal who becomes the clownishly homicidal Joker.

- ☐ **Black Panther (2018):** T'Challa, heir to the hidden but advanced kingdom of Wakanda, must step forward to lead his people into a new future and must confront a challenger from his country's past.

- ☐ **Blade Runner (1982):** A blade runner must pursue and terminate four replicants who stole a ship in space, and have returned to Earth to find their creator. **Goof:** Police these days wear clip-on ties instead of full neckties to prevent culprits from using them to choke cops. Since Deckard is a former cop forced back on the job, it is unlikely that he would have worn a full tie--and wearing a clip-on would have kept Pris from strangling him during their fight.

- ☐ **Brazil (1985):** A bureaucrat in a dystopic society becomes an enemy of the state as he pursues the woman of his dreams.

- ☐ **A Clockwork Orange (1971):** In the future, a sadistic gang leader is imprisoned and volunteers for a conduct-aversion experiment, but it doesn't go as planned. **Fun Fact:** During the filming of the Ludovico scene, star Malcolm McDowell scratched one of his corneas and was temporarily blinded. He suffered cracked ribs during filming of the humiliation stage show.

- ☐ **Close Encounters of the Third Kind (1977):** Roy Neary, an electric lineman, watches how his quiet and ordinary daily life turns upside down after a close encounter with a UFO.

- ☐ **The Dark Knight Franchise (2008):** When the menace known as the Joker wreaks havoc and chaos on the people of Gotham, Batman must accept one of the greatest psychological and physical tests of his ability to fight injustice.

- ☐ **The Day the Earth Stood Still (1951):** An alien lands and tells the people of Earth that they must live peacefully or be destroyed as a danger to other planets. **Fun Fact:** The spaceship was made of wood, wire and plaster of Paris.

☐ **Divergent (2014):** In a world divided by factions based on virtues, Tris learns she's Divergent and won't fit in. When she discovers a plot to destroy Divergents, Tris and the mysterious Four must find out what makes Divergents dangerous before it's too late. I have only included some of these franchises because they had a huge cult following and not necessarily that they are good movies.

☐ **Dr. Strangelove or: How I learned to Stop Worrying and Love the Bomb (1964):** An insane General triggers a path to nuclear holocaust that a War Room full of politicians and generals frantically tries to stop. **Goof:** Even renowned perfectionist Stanley Kubrick was prone to the occasional mistake, including grammatical errors. During the opening credits sequence in this dark comedy, the text reads, "Base on the book *Red Alert* by Peter George." The words "fictitious" and "occurrence" are also misspelled during the same credits sequence. **Memorable Quote:** *"Gentlemen, you can't fight in here! This is the war room!"*

☐ **Edward Scissorhands (1990):** An artificial man, who was incompletely constructed and has scissors for hands, leads a solitary life. Then one day, a suburban lady meets him and introduces him to her world.

☐ **E.T. (1982):** A troubled child summons the courage to help a friendly alien escape Earth and return to his home world. **Memorable Quote:** *"E.T. phone home."*

☐ **Fahrenheit 451 (1966):** In an oppressive future, a fireman whose duty is to destroy all books begins to question his task. **Fun Fact:** The film's credits are spoken, not read, in keeping with the film's theme of destruction of reading material.

☐ **Fantastic Four (2005):** A group of astronauts gain superpowers after a cosmic radiation exposure and must use them to oppose the plans of their enemy, Doctor Victor Von Doom. See above comment about Divergent and others.

☐ **The Fly (1986):** A brilliant but eccentric scientist begins to transform into a giant man/fly hybrid after one of his experiments goes horribly wrong. **Goof:** When Brundlefly dissolves Stathis's hand, a considerable amount of vomit falls on his chest, but there is no sign of any damage unlike his hand and his foot.

☐ **Forbidden Planet (1956):** A starship crew goes to investigate the silence of a planet's colony only to find two survivors and a deadly secret that one of them has.

☐ **Ghostbusters (1984):** Three former parapsychology professors set up shop as a unique ghost removal service. **Fun Fact:** Dan Aykroyd's original script for *Ghostbusters* was set in a future where Ghostbusters were everyday figures of society like paramedics and firemen.

☐ **Harry Potter Franchise (2001):** An orphaned boy enrolls in a school of wizardry, where he learns the truth about himself, his family and the terrible evil that haunts the magical world.

☐ **Hunger Games (2012):** Katniss Everdeen voluntarily takes her younger sister's place in the Hunger Games: a televised competition in which two teenagers from each of the twelve Districts of Panem are chosen at random to fight to the death. **Fun Fact:** On the set of *Hunger Games*, Jennifer Lawrence told co-star Josh Hutcherson she could kick all the way over his head. Instead, she gave him a concussion.

☐ **The Incredible Shrinking Man (1957):** When Scott Carey begins to shrink because of exposure to a combination of radiation and insecticide, medical science is powerless to help him.

☐ **Independence Day (1996):** The aliens are coming and their goal is to invade and destroy Earth. Fighting superior technology, mankind's best weapon is the will to survive.

☐ **Interstellar (2014):** A team of explorers travel through a wormhole in space in an attempt to ensure humanity's survival. **Memorable Quote:** *"We used to look up at the sky and wonder at our place in* *the stars. Now we just look down, and worry about our place in the dirt."*

☐ **Invasion of the Body Snatchers (1956):** A small-town doctor learns that the population of his community is being replaced by emotionless alien duplicates.

☐ **Jurassic Park (1993):** A pragmatic paleontologist visiting an almost complete theme park is tasked with protecting a couple of kids after a power failure causes the park's cloned dinosaurs to run loose. **Fun Fact:** The sounds the Velociraptors make when communicating is the same sound tortoises make when having sex.

☐ **Logan (2017):** In a future where mutants are nearly extinct, an elderly and weary Logan leads a quiet life. But when Laura, a mutant child pursued by scientists, comes to him for help, he must get her to safety.

☐ **Mad Max Franchise (1979):** In a self-destructing world, a vengeful Australian policeman sets out to stop a violent motorcycle gang. **My Two Cents:** This is one where the sequel is actually better than the first.

☐ **The Man in the White Suit (1951):** An altruistic chemist invents a fabric which resists wear and stain as a boon to humanity, but big business and labor realize it must be suppressed for economic reasons.

☐ **The Matrix (1999):** A computer hacker learns from mysterious rebels about the true nature of his reality and his role in the war against its controllers. **Fun Fact:** Kung Fu choreographer Woo-Ping Yuen initially refused to work on the film, and hoped that by asking for an exorbitant fee, it would turn off the Wachowskis. It didn't. He next formulated what he considered an impossible request. He said that he'd agree only if he had complete control of the fights, and that he trained the actors for four months before they shoot. The Wachowskis complied with his request. **Fun Fact:** The Matrix code actually comes from a sushi cookbook.

☐ **Men in Black (1997):** A police officer joins a secret organization that polices and monitors extraterrestrial interactions on Earth.

☐ **Minority Report (2002):** In a future where a special police unit is able to arrest murderers before they commit their crimes, an officer from that unit is himself accused of a future murder.

☐ **Planet of the Apes (1968):** An astronaut crew crash-lands on a planet in the distant future where intelligent talking apes are the dominant species, and humans are the oppressed and enslaved. **Misquote:** "Get your stinking paws off me, you damn dirty ape." **Actual Quote:** "*Take* your stinking paws off me, you damn dirty ape."

☐ **Resident Evil Franchise (2002):** A special military unit fights a powerful, out-of-control supercomputer and hundreds of scientists who have mutated into flesh-eating creatures after a laboratory accident.

☐ **RoboCop (1987):** In a dystopic and crime-ridden Detroit, a terminally wounded cop returns to the force as a powerful cyborg haunted by submerged memories.

☐ **Spider-Man Franchise (2002):** When bitten by a genetically modified spider, a nerdy, shy, and awkward high school student gains spider-like abilities that he eventually must use to fight evil as a superhero after tragedy befalls his family. **Goof:** When Peter is trying to figure out how to shoot his web across to the crane, there is a billboard that says tune into 98.8 FM. In the United States, FM radio stations do not end in even numbers.

☐ **Star Trek (1979):** When an alien spacecraft of enormous power is spotted approaching Earth, Admiral James T. Kirk resumes command of the overhauled USS Enterprise in order to intercept it.

☐ **Star Wars Franchise (1977):** Luke Skywalker joins forces with a Jedi Knight, a cocky pilot, a Wookiee and two droids to save the galaxy from the Empire's world-destroying battle station, while also attempting to rescue Princess Leia from the mysterious Darth

Vader. **Fun Fact:** George Lucas' dog inspired Chewbacca. **Fun Fact:** Like Facebook, *Star Wars* was originally prefixed by the definite article 'The.' Much cleaner without it. **Memorable Quote:** *"May the Force be with you."* **Memorable Quote:** *"Help me, Obi-Wan Kenobi. You're my only hope."*

☐ **Superman (1978):** An alien orphan is sent from his dying planet to Earth, where he grows up to become his adoptive home's first and greatest superhero.

☐ **The Terminator Franchise (1984):** A human soldier is sent from 2029 to 1984 to stop an almost indestructible cyborg killing machine, sent from the same year, which has been programmed to execute a young woman whose unborn son is the key to humanity's future salvation. **Fun Fact:** One afternoon during a break in filming, Arnold Schwarzenegger went into a restaurant in downtown L.A. to get some lunch and realized all too late that he was still in Terminator makeup - with a missing eye, exposed jawbone and burned flesh. **Fun Fact:** Arnold Schwarzenegger worked with guns every day for a month to prepare for the role. The first two weeks of filming he practiced weapons stripping and reassembly blindfolded until the motions were automatic, like a machine. He spent hours at the shooting range and practicing with different weapons without blinking or looking at them when reloading or cocking. He also had to be ambidextrous. **Fun Fact:** O.J. Simpson was considered for the Terminator, but the producers feared he was "too nice" to be taken seriously as a cold-blooded killer. **Memorable Quote:** *"I'll be back."* **My Favorite Line:** *"Hasta la vista, baby."*

☐ **Time Bandits (1981):** A young boy accidentally joins a band of time travelling dwarves, as they jump from era to era looking for treasure to steal.

☐ **Tomb Raider (2001):** Video game adventurer Lara Croft comes to life in a movie where she races against time and villains to recover powerful ancient artifacts. **Fun Fact:** Filming the scenes where Lara drives her Land Rover through the jungle there had to be endless re-shoots due to snakes and other wildlife falling through the open top roof. Angelina Jolie herself was reported to be terrified.

☐ **Total Recall (1990):** When a man goes in to have virtual vacation memories of the planet Mars implanted in his mind, an unexpected and harrowing series of events forces him to go to the planet for real - or is he?

☐ **Tron (1982):** A computer hacker is abducted into the digital world and forced to participate in gladiatorial games where his only chance of escape is with the help of a heroic security program.

☐ **Twelve Monkeys (1995):** In a future world devastated by disease, a convict is sent back in time to gather information about the man-made virus that wiped out most of the human population on the planet. **Memorable Quote:** *"There's no right, there's no wrong, there's only popular opinion."*

☐ **Underworld (2003):** Selene, a vampire warrior, is entrenched in a conflict between vampires and werewolves, while falling in love with Michael, a human who is sought by werewolves for unknown reasons.

☐ **War of the Worlds (1953):** A small town in California is attacked by Martians, beginning a worldwide invasion.

☐ **Westworld (1973):** A robot malfunction creates havoc and terror for unsuspecting vacationers at a futuristic, adult-themed amusement park. **Goof:** Footprints, unless they are left by bare or stocking feet, would be the same temperature as the ambient air. That means it would be useless trying to track someone from their "temperature."

☐ **X-Men (2000):** In a world where mutants (evolved super-powered humans) exist and are discriminated against, two groups form for an inevitable clash: the supremacist Brotherhood, and the pacifist X-Men.

□ **2001: A Space Odyssey (1968):** After discovering a mysterious artifact buried beneath the Lunar surface, mankind sets off on a quest to find its origins with help from intelligent supercomputer H.A.L. 9000. **Fun Fact:** Stanley Kubrick destroyed almost all of his props and sets from *2001: A Space Odyssey* because he didn't want them to be used in any lesser science fiction films.

Sports

This probably isn't a real genre that should be specified, but I put it in here anyways, because I freaking love sports and feel-good comeback stories.

☐ **Ali (2001):** A biography of sports legend Muhammad Ali, focusing on his triumphs and controversies between 1964 and 1974.

☐ **All the Right Moves (1983):** An ambitious young football star is trapped in a dying mill town--unless his gridiron skills can win him a way out.

☐ **Angels in the Outfield (1994):** When a boy prays for a chance to have a family if the California Angels win the pennant, angels are assigned to make that possible. **Best Song:** "Hippy Hippy Shake"

☐ **Any Given Sunday (1999):** A behind-the-scenes look at the life-and-death struggles of modern-day gladiators and those who lead them.

☐ **The Bad News Bears (1976):** An aging, down-on-his-luck ex-minor leaguer coaches a team of misfits in an ultra-competitive California little league.

☐ **The Basketball Diaries (1995):** A teenager finds his dreams of becoming a basketball star threatened after he free falls into the harrowing world of drug addiction. **Goof:** The NBA ball signed by the players would not have been around at that time. Spalding didn't start manufacturing the NBA ball until 1982 or 1983.

☐ **The Big Green (1995):** A teacher on exchange from England is placed in an underachieving Texan school, where she coaches the children in soccer, improving their self-esteem and leading to unexpected success.

☐ **The Blind Side (2009):** The story of Michael Oher, a homeless and traumatized boy who became an All-American football player and first-round NFL draft pick with the help of a caring woman and her family.

☐ **Blue Chips (1994):** A college basketball coach is forced to break the rules in order to get the players he needs to stay competitive. **Fun Fact:** Nick Nolte wrote a 200-page novel about Pete Bell to tap into the character's psyche.

☐ **Blue Crush (2002):** As a hard-core surfer girl prepares for a big competition, she finds herself falling for a football player.

☐ **Bring It On (2000):** A champion high school cheerleading squad discovers its previous captain stole all their best routines from an inner-city school and must scramble to compete at this year's championships.

☐ **Bull Durham (1988):** A fan who has an affair with one minor-league baseball player each season meets an up-and-coming pitcher and the experienced catcher assigned to him. **Goof:** At the time of the film's release, the Durham Bulls were the Single A affiliate of the Atlanta Braves but there is never any mention of this.

☐ **Cinderella Man (2005):** The story of James J. Braddock, a supposedly washed-up boxer who came back to challenge for the heavyweight championship of the world.

☐ **Coach Carter (2005):** Controversy surrounds high school basketball coach Ken Carter after he benches his entire team for breaking their academic contract with him.

☐ **The Color of Money (1986):** Fast Eddie Felson teaches a cocky but immensely talented protégé the ropes of pool hustling, which in turn inspires him to make an unlikely comeback. **Memorable Quote:** *"Money won is twice as sweet as money earned."*

☐ **Cool Runnings (1993):** When a Jamaican sprinter is disqualified from the Olympic Games, he enlists the help of a dishonored coach to start the first Jamaican Bobsled Team.

☐ **Days of Thunder (1990):** A young hot-shot stock car driver gets his chance to compete at the top level. **Fun Fact:** According to Dale Earnhardt, Jr., Tom Cruise had a meeting with Dale Earnhardt, Sr. prior to the production of the film. It was rumored that Earnhardt was offered the role of Rowdy Burns, but he turned it down because he did not want to play the bad guy.

☐ **Dogtown and Z-Boys (2001):** Documentary about the pioneering 1970s Zephyr skating team.

☐ **Field of Dreams (1989):** Iowa farmer Ray Kinsella is inspired by a voice he can't ignore to pursue a dream he can hardly believe. Supported by his wife, Ray begins the quest by turning his ordinary cornfield into a place where dreams can come true. **Misquote:** "If you build it, they will come." **Actual Quote:** "If you build it, *he* will come."

☐ **The Fighter (2010):** Based on the story of Micky Ward, a fledgling boxer who tries to escape the shadow of his more famous but troubled older boxing brother and get his own shot at greatness.

☐ **Greater (2016):** The story of Brandon Burlsworth, possibly the greatest walk-on in the history of college football.

☐ **Happy Gilmore (1996):** A rejected hockey player puts his skills to the golf course to save his grandmother's house. **Fun Fact:** When Dennis Dugan told Bob Barker that a stunt double would be used in the fight scene, Barker insisted on doing his own stunts, saying, "Wait a minute, I know how to fight."

☐ **Hoop Dreams (1994):** A film following the lives of two inner-city Chicago boys who struggle to become college basketball players on the road to going professional.

☐ **Hoosiers (1986):** A coach with a checkered past and a local drunk train a small-town high school basketball team to become a top contender for the championship.

☐ **The Hustler (1961):** An up-and-coming pool player plays a long-time champion in a single high-stakes match. **Fun Fact:** One of the first mainstream Hollywood films to use the word "bastard."

☐ **Invictus (2009):** Nelson Mandela, in his first term as President of South Africa, initiates a unique venture to unite the Apartheid-torn land: enlist the national rugby team on a mission to win the 1995 Rugby World Cup.

☐ **Jerry Maguire (1996):** When a sports agent has a moral epiphany and is fired for expressing it, he decides to put his new philosophy to the test as an independent agent with the only athlete who stays with him and his former colleague. **Memorable Quote:** *"You complete me."* **Memorable Quote:** *"Show me the money!"* **My Favorite Line:** *"You had me at Hello."*

☐ **Kingpin (1996):** A star bowler whose career was prematurely "cut off" hopes to ride a new prodigy to success and riches.

☐ **The Longest Yard (1976):** A sadistic warden asks a former pro quarterback, now serving time in his prison, to put together a team of inmates to take on (and get pummeled by) the guards.

☐ **Love and Basketball (2000):** Monica and Quincy love and play basketball together through many life challenges from childhood to adulthood. **Memorable Quote:** *"I've been in love with you since I was eleven, and the shit won't go away."*

☐ **Major League (1989):** The new owner of the Cleveland Indians puts together a purposely horrible team so they'll lose and she can move the team. But when the plot is uncovered, they start winning just to spite her. **Best Song:** "Wild Thing"

☐ **The Mighty Ducks (1992):** A self-centered Minnesota lawyer is sentenced to community service coaching a rag tag youth hockey team. **My Two Cents:** I also love D2, I ruined many videotapes watching that movie, I had a crush on the dude from Iceland.

☐ **Miracle (2004):** The true story of Herb Brooks, the player-turned-coach who led the 1980 U.S. Olympic hockey team to victory over the seemingly invincible Soviet squad.

☐ **Moneyball (2011):** Oakland A's general manager Billy Beane's successful attempt to assemble a baseball team on a lean budget by employing computer-generated analysis to acquire new players. **Fun Fact:** Since there was no money to shoot in all the stadiums the Oakland Athletics visited, Dodger Stadium was dressed up as eight different ballparks.

☐ **The Natural (1984):** A middle-aged unknown comes seemingly out of nowhere to become a legendary baseball player with almost supernatural talent.

☐ **Pride of the Yankees (1942):** The story of the life and career of famed baseball player Lou Gehrig. **Memorable Quote:** *"Today, I consider myself the luckiest man on the face of the earth."*

☐ **Radio (2003):** The story of a high school coach and the developmentally challenged man who he took under his wing.

☐ **Remember the Titans (2000):** The true story of a newly appointed African-American coach and his high school team on their first season as a racially integrated unit.

☐ **Rookie of the Year (1993):** When an accident miraculously gives a boy an incredibly powerful pitching arm, he becomes a major league pitcher for the Chicago Cubs. **Goof:** A player may not be signed to a major league team until he is 16 years old. The filmmakers obviously chose to ignore this, otherwise there would be no movie.

☐ **Rudy (1993):** Rudy has always been told that he was too small to play college football. But he is determined to overcome the odds and fulfill his dream of playing for Notre Dame.

☐ **Rush (2013):** The merciless 1970s rivalry between Formula One rivals James Hunt and Niki Lauda.

☐ **The Sandlot (1993):** In the summer of 1962, a new kid in town is taken under the wing of a young baseball prodigy and his rowdy team, resulting in many adventures. **My Favorite Line:** *"You're killin' me, Smalls."*

☐ **Seabiscuit (2003):** True story of the undersized Depression-era racehorse whose victories lifted not only the spirits of the team behind it but also those of their nation.

☐ **Tin Cup (1996):** A washed up golf pro working at a driving range tries to qualify for the US Open in order to win the heart of his successful rival's girlfriend.

☐ **Varsity Blues (1999):** A back-up quarterback is chosen to lead a Texas football team to victory after the star quarterback is injured. **Best Song: "**Thunderstruck"

☐ **Vision Quest (1985):** A high school wrestler in Spokane, Washington has trouble focusing on his training regimen when a beautiful young drifter takes up temporary residence at his home.

☐ **Warrior (2011):** The youngest son of an alcoholic former boxer returns home, where he's trained by his father for competition in a mixed martial arts tournament - a path that puts the fighter on a collision course with his estranged, older brother.

☐ **The Way Back (2020):** Jack Cunningham was a high school basketball phenom who walked away from the game, forfeiting his future. Years later, when he reluctantly accepts a coaching job at his alma mater, he may get one last shot at redemption. **Memorable Quote:** *"You want to know why they're leaving you open? It's because they don't think you can hit the ocean from the beach."*

☐ **We are Marshall (2006):** When a plane crash claims the lives of members of the Marshall University football team and some of its fans, the team's new coach and his surviving players try to keep the football program alive.

☐ **White Men Can't Jump (1992):** Black and white basketball hustlers join forces to double their chances of winning money on the street courts and in a basketball tournament.

☐ **The Wrestler (2008):** A faded professional wrestler must retire, but finds his quest for a new life outside the ring a dispiriting struggle. **Fun Fact:** Due to the film's modest budget, Axl Rose donated the use of Guns N' Roses' "Sweet Child O' Mine" free of charge for the final match.

☐ **Youngblood (1986):** A 17-year-old farm boy is offered an ice hockey tryout. His brother drives him to Canada. He has fast legs, slow fists, but is chosen. Will he learn to use his fists and play ice hockey the Canuck way? Will he get the coach's cute daughter?

Teen Angst

Oh, our teen years, some of the best years in our lives, and most, felt like some of the worst. I was semi-quiet in high school and never dated. I had an obsession with Britney Spears and knew all of her dance moves. Yes, I was a virgin when I graduated high school, but whateves, it's not a bad thing. One of the first movies I wrote when I was a teen was about a high school show choir. I am fully convinced someone heard about this when I was an extra on movie sets and made the show *Glee*.

☐ **Adventures in Babysitting (1987):** A babysitter must battle her way through the big city after being stranded there with the kids she's looking after.

☐ **American Graffiti (1973):** A couple of high school grads spend one final night cruising the strip with their buddies before they go off to college.

☐ **American Pie (1999):** Four teenage boys enter a pact to lose their virginity by prom night. **My Two Cents:** One of the popular guys in high school said I was totally the modest girl who would then say she stuck a flute up her pussy…awesome…now I write about sex, go figure.

☐ **Big (1988):** After wishing to be made big, a teenage boy wakes the next morning to find himself mysteriously in the body of an adult.

☐ **Bill and Ted's Excellent Adventure (1989):** Two seemingly dumb teens set off on a quest to prepare the ultimate historical presentation with the help of a time machine.

☐ **Blockers (2018):** Three parents try to stop their daughters from losing their virginity on prom night. **Fun Fact:** The film was originally titled *Cherries* during development in 2012. When production began, it was changed to *The Pact*. It was renamed *Blockers* in October 2017, when the film was in post-production and the first trailer was released.

☐ **The Breakfast Club (1985):** Five high school students meet in Saturday detention and discover they have a lot more in common than they thought. **Best Scene:** When Bender gets all those detentions. **Best Song:** "Don't You (Forget About Me)"

☐ **But I'm a Cheerleader (1999):** A naive teenager is sent to rehab camp when her straitlaced parents and friends suspect her of being a lesbian.

☐ **Can't Buy Me Love (1987):** An outcast secretly pays the most popular girl in school one thousand dollars to pretend to be his girlfriend for a month.

☐ **Can't Hardly Wait (1998):** A complete graduating class, consisting of beautiful girls, geeks and promising footballers, assemble at a rich classmate's residence for a party. Interesting developments follow at the get-together. **Fun Fact:** Melissa Joan Hart was in the middle of filming the 2nd season of *Sabrina the Teenage Witch* (1996) at the same time. She took B12 vitamins to stay energized during the all-night shoots. Jennifer Love Hewitt was skeptical when Hart offered them to her, because she was convinced they were drugs.

☐ **Clueless (1995):** A rich high school student tries to boost a new pupil's popularity, but reckons without affairs of the heart getting in the way. **My Favorite Line:** *"As if!"*

☐ **Cruel Intentions (1999):** Two vicious step-siblings of an elite Manhattan prep school make a wager: to deflower the new headmaster's daughter before the start of term.

☐ **Don't Tell Mom the Babysitter's Dead (1991):** Five siblings are left alone all summer when their mom leaves town and the evil babysitter bites the dust. **My Favorite Line:** *"I'm right on top of that, Rose."*

☐ **The Duff (2015):** A high school senior instigates a social pecking order revolution after finding out that she has been labeled the DUFF - Designated Ugly Fat Friend - by her prettier, more popular counterparts.

☐ **Easy A (2010):** A clean-cut high school student relies on the school's rumor mill to advance her social and financial standing.

☐ **The Edge of Seventeen (2016):** High-school life gets even more unbearable for Nadine when her best friend, Krista, starts dating her older brother. **Memorable Quote:** *"There are two types of people in the world: The people who naturally excel at life. And the people who hope all those people die in a big explosion."*

☐ **Election (1999):** A high school teacher meets his match in an over-achieving student politician.

☐ **Fast Times at Richmond High (1982):** A group of Southern California high school students are enjoying their most important subjects: sex, drugs, and rock n' roll.

☐ **The Faults in Our Stars (2014):** Two teenage cancer patients begin a life-affirming journey to visit a reclusive author in Amsterdam. **Fun Fact:** Shailene Woodley cut her waist-long hair, which she needs for her role as Tris in *Insurgent*, to a pageboy haircut and was not able to wear a wig. She donated the hair to a local children's hospital that makes wigs for the kids.

☐ **Ferris Bueller's Day off (1986):** A high school wise guy is determined to have a day off from school, despite what the principal thinks of that. **Fun Fact:** Bueller? Bueller? Bueller? Cruise? Cusack? Carrey? Depp? All were considered for the part of the hooky playing teen. **Fun Fact:** For his scene in *Ferris Bueller's Day Off* Charlie Sheen stayed awake for 48 hours to give the desired 'wasted' look. To produce the look for his actual life Charlie Sheen hasn't slept in 14 years.

☐ **Freaky Friday (1976):** A mother and daughter find their personalities switched and have to live each other's lives on one strange Friday.

☐ **Heathers (1989):** At Westerburg High where cliques rule, jocks dominate and all the popular girls are named Heather, it's going to take a Veronica and mysterious new kid to give teen angst a body count.

☐ **John Tucker Must Die (2006):** Three ex-girlfriends of a serial cheater set up their former lover to fall for the new girl in town so they can watch him get his heart broken. **Fun Fact:** Arielle Kebbel improvised the line "slut in truck!" on the spot.

☐ **Love, Simon (2018):** Simon Spier keeps a huge secret from his family, his friends and all of his classmates: he's gay. When that secret is threatened, Simon must face everyone and come to terms with his identity.

☐ **Mean Girls (2004):** Cady Heron is a hit with The Plastics, the A-list girl clique, until she makes the mistake of falling for Aaron Samuels, the ex-boyfriend of alpha Plastic Regina George. **My Favorite Line:** *"Gretchen, stop trying to make fetch happen! It's not going to happen!"*

☐ **Napoleon Dynamite (2004):** A listless and alienated teenager decides to help his new friend win the class presidency in their small western high school, while he must deal with his bizarre family life back home. **Fun Fact:** Jon Heder was paid $1,000 to play Napoleon Dynamite. The movie grossed over $40,000,000 in the United States.

☐ **Never Been Kissed (1999):** A newspaper reporter enrolls in high school as part of research for a story. **My Two Cents:** Had the biggest crush on Guy…There was someone that looked similar to him at one of the rivaling schools and he would just give me goosebumps.

☐ **Nick and Norah's Infinite Playlist (2008):** High school student Nick O'Leary, member of the Queercore band The Jerk Offs, meets college-bound Norah Silverberg when she asks him to be her boyfriend for five minutes.

☐ **Not Another Teen Movie (2001):** A sendup of all the teen movies that have accumulated in the past two decades.

☐ **Now and Then (1995):** Four 12-year-old girls grow up together during an eventful small-town summer in 1970. **Goof:** In the movie they say that their home town is Shelby, Indiana. Shelby, Indiana is in the north western part of Indiana. They went to Greenfield, Indiana to go to the library, on their bikes. That is impossible: they are approx. 150 miles apart.

☐ **The Outsiders (1983):** The rivalry between two gangs, the poor Greasers and the rich Socs, only heats up when one gang member kills a member of the other.

☐ **The Perks of Being a Wallflower (2012):** An introvert freshman is taken under the wings of two seniors who welcome him to the real world.

☐ **Pitch Perfect (2012):** Beca, a freshman at Barden University, is cajoled into joining The Bellas, her school's all-girls singing group. Injecting some much-needed energy into their repertoire, The Bellas take on their male rivals in a campus competition. **Fun Fact:** During the Riff-Off, Ester Dean sings "S&M," which was co-written by her.

☐ **Pretty in Pink (1986):** A poor girl must choose between the affections of dating her childhood sweetheart or a rich but sensitive playboy. **My Two Cents:** I think her dress is terrible.

☐ **Pump up the Volume (1990):** Mark runs a pirate radio station and causes an uproar when he speaks his mind and enthralls fellow teens.

☐ **Revenge of the Nerds (1984):** At Adams College, a group of bullied outcasts and misfits resolve to fight back for their peace and self-respect.

☐ **Say Anything (1989):** A noble underachiever and a beautiful valedictorian fall in love the summer before she goes off to college. **Best Scene:** The boombox…c'mon, guys need to amp up their game.

☐ **Scott Pilgrim vs. the World (2010):** In a magically realistic version of Toronto, a young man must defeat his new girlfriend's seven evil exes one by one in order to win her heart.

☐ **She's All That (1999):** A high school jock makes a bet that he can turn an unattractive girl into the school's prom queen. **My Two Cents:** My love for Paul Walker begins. **Best Song:** "The Rockafeller Skank"

☐ **She's the Man (2006):** When her brother decides to ditch for a couple weeks, Viola heads over to his elite boarding school, disguised as him, and proceeds to fall for his school's star soccer player, and soon learns she's not the only one with romantic troubles.

☐ **Sixteen Candles (1984):** A girl's "sweet" sixteenth birthday becomes anything but special when she suffers from every embarrassment possible. **My Two Cents**: Jack Ryan, that is all. **My Favorite Line:** *"I can't believe they fucking forgot my birthday."*

☐ **Some Kind of Wonderful (1987):** When Keith goes out with Amanda, the girl of his dreams, Amanda's ex-boyfriend plans to get back at Keith. Meanwhile, Keith's best friend, tomboy Watts, realizes she has feelings for Keith. **Memorable Quote:** *"You look good wearing my future."*

☐ **Step Up (2006):** Tyler Gage receives the opportunity of a lifetime after vandalizing a performing arts school, gaining him the chance to earn a scholarship and dance with an up-and-coming dancer, Nora.

☐ **Superbad (2007):** Two co-dependent high school seniors are forced to deal with separation anxiety after their plan to stage a booze-soaked party goes awry. **Fun Fact:** Writers Seth Rogen and Evan Goldberg started this script when they were just thirteen years old, because "we just wanted to see if we could write a movie."

☐ **Teen Wolf (1985):** An ordinary high school student discovers that his family has an unusual pedigree when he finds himself turning into a werewolf.

☐ **To All the Boys I've Loved Before (2018):** A teenage girl's secret love letters are exposed and wreak havoc on her love life.

☐ **Valley Girl (1983):** Julie, a girl from the valley, meets Randy, a punk from the city. They are from different worlds and find love. Somehow they need to stay together in spite of her trendy, shallow friends. **My Two Cents:** My mom's favorite teen movie, so you guessed it, had to put it on the list.

☐ **A Walk to Remember (2002):** The story of two North Carolina teens, Landon Carter and Jamie Sullivan, who are thrown together after Landon gets into trouble and is made to do community service.

☐ **10 Things I Hate About You (1999):** A pretty, popular teenager isn't allowed to go out on a date until her ill-tempered older sister does.

☐ **17 Again (2009):** Mike O'Donnell is ungrateful for how his life turned out. He gets a chance to rewrite his life when he tried to save a janitor near a bridge and jumped after him into a time vortex. **Goof:** When 17-year-old Mike is dancing with the cheerleaders in 1989, the coach calls him Vanilla Ice, who didn't make it big until 1990-1991.

☐ **21 Jump Street (2012):** A pair of underachieving cops are sent back to a local high school to blend in and bring down a synthetic drug ring.

War/Western

And last and definitely least is the War/Western genre. I only included what I thought would be the best that is why there is only 25, I am not a huge fan of this genre and I am guessing most of you will feel the same.

☐ **Apocalypse Now (1979):** A U.S. Army officer serving in Vietnam is tasked with assassinating a renegade Special Forces Colonel who sees himself as a god. **Misquote:** "I love the smell of napalm in the morning. It smells like victory!" **Actual Quote:** "I love the smell of napalm in the morning. *You know, one time we had a hill bombed for 12 hours. When it was all over, I walked up. We didn't find one of 'em, not one stinkin' dink body. The smell, you know, that gasoline smell, the whole hill.* Smells like victory." **Fun Fact:** Francis Ford Coppola would read passages of *Heart of Darkness* to Marlon Brando on the fractious set of *Apocalypse Now* after learning the actor had never read the source material. **Goof:** Making this Vietnam War epic was an absolute nightmare for director Francis Ford Coppola, so it's no surprise that the film contains a reported 395 errors. During one of the movie's most iconic scenes, "Ride of the Valkyries" plays through aerial speakers as military helicopters approach a small village. A closer look reveals that the reel-to-reel tape never touches the playback head.

☐ **Black Hawk Down (2001):** 160 elite U.S. soldiers drop into Somalia to capture two top lieutenants of a renegade warlord and find themselves in a desperate battle with a large force of heavily-armed Somalis.

☐ **Catch-22 (1970):** A man is trying desperately to be certified insane during World War II, so he can stop flying missions.

☐ **The Dirty Dozen (1967):** During World War II, a rebellious U.S. Army Major is assigned a dozen convicted murderers to train and lead them into a mass assassination mission of German officers. **Goof:** Several times the characters fire their M3 Grease Guns with the dust cover closed. The dust cover doubled as the safety on those weapons and it would never fire with it closed.

☐ **Dunkirk (2017):** Allied soldiers from Belgium, the British Commonwealth and Empire, and France are surrounded by the German Army and evacuated during a fierce battle in World War II.

☐ **For a Few Dollars More (1965):** Two bounty hunters with the same intentions team up to track down a Western outlaw.

☐ **Full Metal Jacket (1987):** A pragmatic U.S. Marine observes the dehumanizing effects the Vietnam War has on his fellow recruits from their brutal boot camp training to the bloody street fighting in Hue.

☐ **Good Morning, Vietnam (1987):** In 1965, an unorthodox and irreverent DJ named Adrian Cronauer begins to shake up things when he is assigned to the U.S. Armed Services radio station in Vietnam. **Memorable Quote:** *"Good morning, Vietnam!"*

☐ **The Good, the Bad, and the Ugly (1966):** A bounty hunting scam joins two men in an uneasy alliance against a third in a race to find a fortune in gold buried in a remote cemetery. **Fun Fact:** The bridge blown up by Eli Wallach and Clint Eastwood in *The Good, The Bad and The Ugly* was prematurely detonated by a Spanish Army Captain. Upon learning of his mistake, the captain ordered his troops to rebuild the bridge, only for it to suffer another explosion once complete. **Goof:** This film makes several major historical errors. In one scene, for example, the Union army flies a flag with 50 stars at a time when the U.S. was only comprised of 34 states. In another, Clint Eastwood and gang blow up a bridge with dynamite or TNT, neither of which were invented before the close of the Civil War.

☐ **The Great Escape (1963):** Allied prisoners of war plan for several hundred of their number to escape from a German camp during World War II.

☐ **Inglorious Basterds (2009):** In Nazi-occupied France during World War II, a plan to assassinate Nazi leaders by a group of Jewish U.S. soldiers coincides with a theatre owner's vengeful plans for the same.

☐ **Judgment at Nuremberg (1961):** In 1948, an American court in occupied Germany tries four Nazis judged for war crimes. **Memorable Quote:** *"We must forget if we want to go on living."*

☐ **The Last of the Mohicans (1992):** Three trappers protect the daughters of a British Colonel in the midst of the French and Indian War.

☐ **Letters from Iwo Jima (2006):** The story of the battle of Iwo Jima between the United States and Imperial Japan during World War II, as told from the perspective of the Japanese who fought it.

☐ **The Magnificent Seven (1960):** Seven gunfighters are hired by Mexican peasants to liberate their village from oppressive bandits. **Fun Fact:** It was Yul Brynner who approached producer Walter Mirisch with the idea of doing a Western adaptation of Akira Kurosawa's classic, *Seven Samurai* (1954).

☐ **M*A*S*H (1970):** The staff of a Korean War field hospital use humor and high jinks to keep their sanity in the face of the horror of war.

☐ **My Darling Clementine (1946):** After their cattle are stolen and their brother murdered, the Earp brothers have a score to settle with the Clanton family.

☐ **Once Upon a Time in the West (1968):** A mysterious stranger with a harmonica joins forces with a notorious desperado to protect a beautiful widow from a ruthless assassin working for the railroad. **My Two Cents:** I want Claudia Cardinale's hair, that is all.

☐ **Paths of Glory (1957):** After refusing to attack an enemy position, a general accuses the soldiers of cowardice and their commanding officer must defend them.

☐ **The Red Badge of Courage (1951):** Truncated adaptation of Stephen Crane's novel about a Civil War Union soldier who struggles to find the courage to fight in the heat of battle.

☐ **Saving Private Ryan (1998):** Following the Normandy Landings, a group of U.S. soldiers go behind enemy lines to retrieve a paratrooper whose brothers have been killed in action. **Fun Fact:** Tom Sizemore was battling a drug addiction during production. Steven Spielberg gave him an ultimatum that he would be blood tested on the set every day of filming, and if he failed the test once he would be fired and the part of Horvath would be recast and re-shot with someone else, even if it was at the end of production.

☐ **She Wore a Yellow Ribbon (1949):** Captain Nathan Brittles, on the eve of retirement, takes out a last patrol to stop an impending massive Indian attack. Encumbered by women who must be evacuated, Brittles finds his mission imperiled.

☐ **They Were Expendable (1945):** A Navy commander fights to prove the battle-worthiness of the PT boat at the start of World War II.

☐ **Tombstone (1993):** A successful lawman's plans to retire anonymously in Tombstone, Arizona is disrupted by the kind of outlaws he was famous for eliminating. **Goof:** Boot Hill Cemetery was not in the town. It's a mile away and it is not on flat ground. They never had them in town due to diseases.

☐ **Tora! Tora! Tora! (1970):** The story of the 1941 Japanese air raid on Pearl Harbor, and the series of preceding American blunders that aggravated its effectiveness.

☐ **True Grit (1969):** A drunken, hard-nosed U.S. Marshal and a Texas Ranger help a stubborn teenager track down her father's murderer in Indian Territory.

☐ **Young Guns (1998):** A group of young gunmen, led by Billy the Kid, become deputies to avenge the murder of the rancher who became their benefactor. But when Billy takes their authority too far, they become the hunted. **Fun Fact:** Charlie Sheen was reportedly a terrible horse rider. He couldn't keep his balance on the horse and fell off several times. His horse took off after the shoot-out with Henry Hill, and he had no clue how to make it stop.

☐ **Zero Dark Thirty (2012):** A chronicle of the decade-long hunt for al-Qaeda terrorist leader Osama bin Laden after the September 2001 attacks, and his death at the hands of the Navy S.E.A.L.s Team 6 in May 2011.

☐ **3.10 to Yuma (2007):** A small-time rancher agrees to hold a captured outlaw who's awaiting a train to go to court in Yuma. A battle of wills ensues as the outlaw tries to psych out the rancher. **Memorable Quote:** *"Sometimes a man has to be big enough to see how small he is."*

☐ **1917 (2019):** April 6th, 1917. As a regiment assembles to wage war deep in enemy territory, two soldiers are assigned to race against time and deliver a message that will stop 1,600 men from walking straight into a deadly trap.

Other Books by Sarah Melland

THE BREAKUP BAND AID/THE BREAKUP BAND AID WORKBOOK

This "How Not To" book gives you everything you supposedly need in a breakup book. Plus, helpful insights as to how not to have a nervous breakdown or a restraining order. It will make you laugh out loud, cry uncontrollable tears, get in shape, travel around the world, and make you glow like the shining confident person you were always meant to be.

PRACTICING LOVE/JOURNAL EDITION

Practicing Love will help you meditate with ease, turn your mind off to distractions, and open your world of possibilities with easy tips you can incorporate into your everyday busy life. It goes into depth about how the ego makes you operate out of fear and shows you how to turn that negative mindset into one that empowers you to conquer obstacles by getting out of your comfort zone. It goes through simple descriptions of all the universal laws that will help you live a more positive, happy, and fulfilled life. It gives you hundreds of affirmations you can recite when you are feeling down in any scenario. It will also show you which words you need to eliminate from your vocabulary immediately and how to start talking in manifestation mode 24/7. It has tons of exercises to help you live in the present moment, become more patient, support yourself in forgiving yourself and others, become less selfish, not react out of judgement, and finally, to always feel unconditionally loved.

PRACTICING LOVE GRATITUDE JOURNAL

Practicing Love Gratitude Journal is 365 days of writing prompts that will take you through all the spiritual laws of attraction and how to show grace in your everyday lives. It allows you to go deep within yourself through daily reflection, shows you what you have been resisting and teaches you how to flip the switch. It will help you heal on numerous levels, relieve stress, anxiety, self-doubt, and ultimately aid in conquering your fears through forgiveness and perseverance. You will create easy, attainable every day goals by setting your intentions and maximizing manifestation throughout the day.

A SINGLE GIRL'S GUIDE TO HILARIOUS FACTS YOU NEVER KNEW ABOUT SEX

Have you ever wondered how many different types of kisses there are? The history of condoms? Fun facts about penises and vaginas? When sex toys were invented? Are you nodding your head to all these questions? If so, this is the book for you. Every single woman should have useless sex facts in her repertoire.

A SINGLE GIRL'S ULTIMATE BUCKET LIST

Have you ever wanted to create your ultimate bucket list? A list of all the things you want to experience in your life, places you want to go, things you want to see... but don't have the time to do the research and put it all together? Well look no further, A Single Girl's Ultimate Bucket List is here. With over 1,000 ideas every woman needs to try at least once in her life, this book is an inspirational must-have, even if you're in a relationship (why should the single girls have all the fun?). A Single Girl's Ultimate Bucket List has everything you need to live your best life and feel accomplished. Enjoy!

www.ingramcontent.com/pod-product-compliance
Lightning Source LLC
Chambersburg PA
CBHW071154180726
48291CB00007B/2448

* 9 7 8 1 7 3 4 6 3 3 3 4 4 *